# A STARRY NIGHT

Matt Hill

Published by Freiling Agency, LLC.

P.O. Box 1264
Warrenton, VA 20188

www.FreilingAgency.com

PB ISBN: 978-1-963701-74-6
HB ISBN: 978-1-963701-75-3
E-book ISBN: 978-1-963701-76-0

# DEDICATION

*To Kelly:*

My bride. My beauty. My heart. Your light is the quiet, patient kind—the kind that doesn't push, but invites. You lead me gently toward the truth I long to remember about myself. You remind me, simply by being you, that love is not something to earn—it's something to remember.

I am, and will forever be, in love with you.

*To my family and friends:*

The ones my soul delights in. Thank you for walking beside me, laughing with me, and holding the mirror steady. May we never grow weary of helping each other remember who we truly are.

And may we always remain in love.

# AUTHOR'S NOTE

This is a spiritual narrative, blending memoir, psychology, and mysticism. While inspired by the public teachings, life experiences, and philosophies of Alfred Adler and Ram Dass, the dialogue and narrative presented in this book are fictionalized and should not be interpreted as direct quotations, endorsements, or representations of their actual words or beliefs.

The characters of Alfred Adler and Ram Dass are respectfully reimagined for the purpose of spiritual and psychological exploration. This book is an independent tribute created with deep admiration and love, and it is not affiliated with, endorsed by, or connected to the Ram Dass Foundation, the estate of Alfred Adler, or any associated organizations.

All teachings and interpretations are offered through the creative lens of the author, who takes full responsibility for the following content.

# WHEN TWO NIGHTS REMEMBERED EACH OTHER

## *About the title and cover art*

✦

When I chose the title *A Starry Night*, I did think of Van Gogh. I've loved his painting for as long as I can remember—its movement, its ache, its sacred disorientation. But I didn't yet know why it belonged to this book.

Not until much later, when I looked again—not at the stars, but at the man behind them.

Van Gogh painted *The Starry Night* from the window of an asylum. He had been cracked open. And from that fracture, gave us something eternal. Not a sky as it appeared—but a sky as it feels when everything false has fallen away.

He seemed to look out at a sky he could never fully explain and tried, instead, to feel it into form. What he created was not a landscape—it was a mirror. Swirling stars, sacred chaos, something that knew him.

Maybe Van Gogh wasn't trying to capture the sky as it looked.

Maybe he was trying to paint the part of himself that longed to dissolve into it.

Not to describe the stars, but to become them.

To lose the self that suffered—and remember the self that *was never separate*.

He once wrote to his brother Theo:

"Why, I ask myself, shouldn't the shining dots of the sky be as accessible as the black dots on the map of France? Just as we take the train to go to Tarascon or Rouen, we take death to reach a star."

He wasn't speaking of death as escape, but as passage. As a return to what is real.

Maybe this book is the answer the painting was waiting for.

Or maybe they were born together, in different centuries, both sent to remind us of the same thing:

Either way, this book is made of the same longing.

I, too, found myself in a kind of asylum—though mine wasn't made of stone. It was built from success, performance, perfection. From roles I had outgrown but didn't know how to shed. And somewhere in the silence between identities, I sat down to write. To listen. To remember.

Like Van Gogh, I wasn't painting what I saw. I was painting what I knew. What I felt. What I had forgotten I was. And by the end, I realized: this was never a book about becoming somebody. It was about laying that down entirely. About remembering we are the sky.

The stars have always been speaking.

This is the night I finally listened.

# A PERSONAL NOTE TO YOU

## *The Reader*

Before the story begins, I want to tell you something.

This isn't just a book.

It's a room.

A sacred one.

There's a fire burning low in the hearth. Two chairs sit across from each other, worn and waiting, and a third—yours—rests between them, angled just so. The walls are lined with books and memory. The window is open just a crack. Outside, stars lean in close, listening. The scent of old cedar and fresh tea weaves through the air like a blessing. The night is thick with presence, and something in you already knows—you're not here by accident.

This is not a story you read *about*.

It's one you *enter*.

You are the narrator. Not just observing from the margins but sitting right there in the silence. You are the one who walked up the hill, stepped through the door, and sat down to listen. And something in you—something deep and remembering—has been waiting for this conversation your whole life.

Ram Dass is here. So is Alfred Adler. Not as distant icons or figures from history, but as living, breathing companions—present and real and impossibly human. They came not to preach, but to wonder. Not to teach from a pedestal, but to sit beside you, to hold up a mirror and ask, softly: *Are you ready to see yourself again?*

This book is not meant to give you answers.

It's meant to undo the questions you never realized were keeping you small.

It's meant to sit with you like an old friend. To knock gently on the walls you've built around your heart. To crack you open in the tenderest places and remind you—slowly, sacredly—that being broken is not the end. It's the doorway.

You'll find no moral to memorize here. No list to follow. No spiritual gold stars to collect.

What you *will* find is space. And warmth. And honesty that burns like truth and feels like love.

And maybe, if you let yourself stay here—really stay—something in you will be seen in a way you've never been seen before. Not the version you've curated, not the identity you've used to earn approval. But *you*. The real you. The soul underneath it all, still intact, still radiant, still quietly waiting to be remembered.

This book is not about Ram Dass or Alfred Adler.

It's about *you*.

The one who has suffered and longed and hidden and hoped. The one who came here not to be inspired, but to *remember*. The one who has always known there is more—more to feel, more to become, more to love.

So come. Bring your questions. Bring your ache. Bring the version of you that has learned to perform and survive—and the one that's ready to live.

There is a seat for you by the fire.

The night is long.

And your soul is ready.

# TABLE OF CONTENTS

# PROLOGUE
## *The Room*

I don't remember how I got here.
Not in the usual sense, anyway.

There was no invitation. No instructions.
Just a feeling—
ancient, familiar.
Like something rising from long ago and
whispering,
*It's time.*

I followed without needing to understand.
And now, I find myself in this room.

Quiet.
Dimly lit.
Timeless.

The walls are old stone—cool to the touch.
The floor creaks gently beneath my steps.
In the center: two wooden chairs, facing each other
across a round table.
A fire crackles in the hearth, its warmth casting
flickering shadows on the walls.
Above it, a kettle hangs suspended from an iron
hook—warming slowly.

There is no urgency here.
Only presence.

A tall, narrow window opens to the darkening sky.
The sun has just slipped below the horizon.
The first stars have begun to appear—
soft pinpricks of light
against the deepening blue.

There's something holy about twilight.
That thin, in-between space.
It feels like a threshold.

I sit near the fire.
Not at the center, but not outside it either.
A wool blanket rests across the arm of the chair.
The scent of cedar smoke, old paper, and something
herbal—
chamomile, maybe—lingers in the air.

The room doesn't ask anything of me.
It simply welcomes.

But still—I feel it.
That pull.
That hush before something begins.
Not the kind of memory that comes from the mind.
Older.
Quieter.
A soul memory.
The kind that settles in the bones.

Something in me remembers this place.
Not the details.
But the feeling.
The knowing.
As if I've been here before.
Sat just like this.
Waiting for something sacred to begin.

The door opens.
Softly.

And the first figure steps inside.

There's something weightless about him—
as though he's here and somewhere else entirely.
He wears robes the color of deep earth.
A soft scarf wraps loosely around his shoulders, too
long on one side.
He pauses to adjust it—fumbling a little—then
shrugs, amused.
His smile isn't blissful.
It's bemused.
Like he's already caught the joke in something we
haven't said yet.

He moves toward the fire, not with reverence, but
with a kind of casual devotion—
like it's an old friend.

Then the second man enters.

His steps are more deliberate.
He closes the door with care, then scans the room

with the quiet calculation of someone who *notices everything*.
He pulls at the cuff of his sleeve once.
Straightens the buttons on his dark wool jacket.
It's not vanity. It's preparation.
He glances at the fire, then at the man already seated.
And for a brief moment—something flickers behind his eyes.
Not recognition.
Relief.

They nod to one another.

Not with formality—
but familiarity.
Like they've met before.
Not in life, maybe—
but in some shared purpose that preceded it.

They don't ask why I'm here.
They don't seem surprised.

It's as if they already know.

They sit.

The fire crackles.
The kettle hums.

And I feel it.
The doorway has opened.

For years, I carried a quiet ache—
not just for meaning,
but for something deeper.
Something more whole.

I was raised in the language of religion,
trained in the habits of achievement.
And somewhere between the two, I lost my place.

I searched for something I could never name—
something between science and spirit,
between truth and tenderness,
between effort and grace.

That search led me to these men.

One walked the path of the soul.
The other, the psyche.

I studied their words in lectures and dog-eared
pages.
Underlined passages at midnight.
Whispered their names like prayers.

And now, here they are.

Ram Dass.
Alfred Adler.

Not theories.
Not relics.
But presence.

Sitting across from one another.
And me.

No one speaks.

But the room has already begun the conversation.

The fire leans forward.
The stars blink.
The kettle begins to stir.

And something ancient inside me
leans in.

# INTRODUCTION
## *Before the Fire*

I didn't find these men in a classroom.
Not really.

I found them in the quiet aftermath of questions I
couldn't answer.
You know the kind—
the ones that show up at 2 a.m.
when achievement feels hollow
and spirituality lacks meaning.
When the performance starts to rot from the inside
out.

Who am I?
Why have I lost all feeling?
What part of me am I afraid to meet?

That's where they found me.
Or maybe that's where I became willing to see them.

Two men—separated by continents and centuries—
each carrying a torch that illuminated something
buried in me.

Ram Dass.
Alfred Adler.

You may not know them.
Or maybe you've only brushed past their names
—in a quote online,
in the footnote of a textbook.

But by the end of this night,
you'll know them as I do.

Not just for what they taught—
but for *who they were.*

Let's start with Adler.

He's often overshadowed by the more well-known
psychiatrists of his time, Sigmund Freud and Carl
Jung.
But Adler was a revolutionary in his own quiet way.

He was born in 1870 in Vienna—
the second of seven children in a family marked by
illness and loss.
He nearly died of pneumonia as a child.
And in a letter later in life, he wrote of lying in bed,
watching dust float in the morning light,
wondering if he would ever grow up.
That's where his hunger came from.
Not to be important—
but to *matter.*

Adler rejected the deterministic view of
psychoanalysis and offered something radical for his
time:

That we are creative beings.
Shaping our lives through the unconscious beliefs
we form in childhood—
beliefs about who we are, and what we must become
to be safe, loved, or seen.

Inferiority wasn't pathology to him.
It was *invitation*.
A spark.
He believed we each create a "lifestyle"—not in the
modern sense, but as a private logic—
a hidden blueprint that governs how we move
through the world.

He taught that healing doesn't happen in isolation,
but in relationship.
Not by dissecting our wounds,
but by reclaiming our *courage to contribute*.

But Adler was not a man untouched by
contradiction.
He had multiple children—and worked constantly.
His life was devoted to ideas, lectures, and shaping
the minds of others.
And though he spoke so often of connection and
belonging,
He once admitted that he felt more at home with his
students
than with his own family.
More known in public than in private.

That line didn't make me trust him less.

It made me exhale.
Because I've known that split too.
The ache of showing up for the world,
While feeling absent in your own home.
Then there was Ram Dass.

If Adler helped me understand my mind,
Ram Dass cracked open my soul.

He was born Richard Alpert in 1931—
a Harvard psychologist. Brilliant. Privileged.
Restless.
In the 1960s, he helped pioneer psychedelic
research.
He once joked that he was "rich in all the ways the
world rewards—
and starved in all the ways that mattered."

When controversy erupted and the academic world
turned on him,
he left it all.
Went to India.
Met a tiny man in a blanket named Neem Karoli
Baba—Maharaji—
who loved him without needing him to be anyone.

Ram Dass said that was the moment his whole
identity shattered.
And something deeper began.

He came back as *Ram Dass*—"servant of God."
But even then, he never claimed to be enlightened.

He once confessed,
"*I still want my guru to show up in dreams and tell me I'm doing it right.*
*I still want a gold star on my spiritual forehead.*"

He laughed when he said it,
But the ache was real.
In his early years of teaching,
He often judged Western seekers who didn't "get it" fast enough.
He rolled his eyes. Looked down.
He carried a quiet superiority—
Mistaking his awakening for a crown.

Until one day, in the middle of a retreat,
He caught himself doing it again.
And it broke him open.

"I was using God to feel better than you," he said.
That's when I knew he was telling the truth.
Ram Dass taught me how to be still.
How to *stop climbing and start listening.*
He reminded me:
"*You don't have to become anything. You already are.*"

Where Adler helped me trace the architecture of my psyche,
Ram Dass helped me fall into the vastness beneath it.

They were different.

Adler wore suits. He lectured in halls.
Ram Dass wore robes. He sat cross-legged and told
jokes that made no sense and healed everything.

One grounded in community and courage.
The other in presence and surrender.

But they weren't opposites.
They were polarity.
A sacred tension.

Adler helped me name the story.
Ram Dass helped me let it go.

And now, here they are.

In this room.
In this story.
With you.

You don't need to know them fully.
Just let them walk with you tonight.

You'll learn who they are through their glances, their
silence, their stray metaphors.
They're not here to impress.
They're here to reveal.

This isn't a textbook.
It isn't a self-help manual.

It's a mirror.

You'll see pieces of yourself in these pages.
In me.
In them.

You might laugh.
You might cry.
You might find a version of yourself
you forgot was still waiting.

Whatever brought you here,
trust that it's enough.

The night is long.
The tea is warm.
The fire is ready.

Let's begin.

# CHAPTER ONE
## *The Room Between Worlds*

The room is still.

A log shifts in the hearth, sending a quiet burst of
sparks upward—
brief light, then smoke.
The fire crackles softly in response,
as if acknowledging the change.

Ram Dass leans forward with a kind of reverence,
adjusting the iron kettle so it hangs a little closer to
the flame.
He doesn't speak.
He doesn't need to.
There's something sacred in the movement.

Adler watches him quietly, his hands resting on his
knees.
His jacket is still buttoned—
though I imagine he'll loosen it once the tea is
poured.
There's a quiet dignity to the way he sits—
upright, composed, present.
Not stiff, just intentional.
Like someone who has practiced being here.

I sit tucked in the corner, the wool blanket drawn up over my legs,
the warmth of the fire settling into my chest.
And yet—beneath the warmth,
there's a quiet tension I can't ignore.
A tightness in my stomach.
A whisper that says:
You are not ready for this.

Outside the window, the last trace of twilight dissolves behind the trees.
Darkness arrives not suddenly, but slowly—
like it's being poured into the sky.
One star, then another.
Then hundreds.
The room shifts with it.
The flickering shadows on the stone walls stretch longer.
The wooden beams seem to creak more deeply—
like they remember stories I've forgotten.

The scent of cedar smoke thickens in the air—
earthy and grounding.
Ram Dass moves with a stillness that feels ancient,
like he's done this before in lifetimes I don't remember.

The kettle hums.
Steam curls upward, catching the firelight like a veil.

The room is more than a room.
It feels like a threshold.

A place between places.
Not fully in this world,
not fully out of it.

And I am not just watching—
I am being watched.
Not by the men.
By the moment.
There is nowhere to hide here.
Not from them.
Not from myself.

A voice inside—quiet but firm—says:

This is it.
The beginning of the undoing.
The beginning of the remembering.

And I haven't even said a word.

∞

The tea hasn't been poured, but something is already
steeping—beneath the surface, beyond thought.
Like this ritual—this simple act of fire and silence—
is preparing more than tea.
It's preparing me.

Outside, the twilight has fully surrendered.
The window reflects the soft glow of stars now,
scattered across a velvet sky.
And in their quiet, unwavering shimmer, I feel

something watching back.
Not judging. Just waiting.

Ram Dass speaks first.
His voice is warm, unhurried, as if it has been forming long before it was spoken.
"Almost ready."

Adler smiles faintly. "Patience, I've learned, is easier to teach than to live."

Ram Dass chuckles softly. "Spoken like a true psychologist."

They exchange a glance. Not dramatic. Just ease.
The kind of look that suggests history, even if that history lives beyond this lifetime.
Two men, rooted in very different worlds, sitting across from one another with a mutual softness I didn't expect.

I study them both.
Ram Dass, wrapped in robes that seem to carry the dust of sacred places.
His presence is like the air before a thunderstorm—charged, yet calm.
Adler, buttoned still, but softened now, like someone who is slowly putting down his armor.
He hasn't removed it, but you can see he's considering it.

They are so different.
And yet—there's something shared.

A familiarity that hums below the surface.
Maybe it's not in the facts of their lives, but in the texture of them.
The ways they've both broken open.
The wounds they've both turned into medicine.

The fire crackles between them like punctuation.
They haven't said much, and yet, the room is full.
Not with noise, but with presence.

I feel it again—that subtle ache in my chest.
Not panic. Not excitement.
Just the faint tug of a soul remembering why it came.

The kettle lets out a low sigh.
And I realize—
Something sacred is already underway.
And I am already part of it.

∞

The kettle begins to whisper.
A low exhale, soft and steady—
like the room itself is breathing.
Ram Dass moves gently, lifting the kettle from the fire with the same quiet reverence he used to place it there.
No one rushes.
Even time feels slower here—
as though it, too, has surrendered to the stillness.

He sets the kettle on a wooden slab beside the table.
Steam rises—

not in a hurry, but in a spiral.
It catches the firelight like incense.
Then he unwraps a small bundle of herbs and loose
tea leaves.
His movements are ceremonial, but not
performative.
This isn't for show.
This is for the soul.

Adler shifts slightly.
Unbuttons his jacket.
Rolls his shoulders back.
And exhales.

The sound is subtle—
but something in the room changes with it.
A release.
A softening.
Like a prayer that doesn't need words.

"I've always admired tea rituals," Adler says, his
voice slow and thoughtful.
"Not for the tea, necessarily. But for what they ask of
us."

Ram Dass raises an eyebrow, already knowing the
answer, but asking anyway.
"And what's that?"

"Slowness," Adler says.
"Stillness. The willingness to let something unfold
without our control."

Ram Dass nods.
"You can't rush it.
You rush, you miss the medicine."

Adler chuckles softly.
"Rather like the soul."

Ram Dass grins.
"Or the psyche."

They both laugh.
Quiet. Warm. Real.
The kind of laughter that doesn't interrupt the moment—
but deepens it.

And I feel it.
The tightness in my body beginning to shift—
not vanish,
but soften.

The way a clenched fist might loosen when someone offers their hand.

I haven't spoken.
But already, I'm being disarmed.
Not by force—
but by presence.

By two minds I once idolized—
now gently teasing each other,
letting the seriousness fall away.

They were once voices in books.
Faces on screens.
Names in footnotes.

Now they are men.
Pouring tea.

And somehow,
that makes me feel more human.
More here.

The leaves steep.
The fire glows.

And I realize—
this night isn't here to impress me.
It's here to open me.

∞

Ram Dass moves with the teapot now,
pouring hot water over a small bundle of loose
leaves he's placed in a clay pot.
The aroma rises—earthy, herbal, slightly sweet.
He sets the lid gently on top and places the pot
between them.
No one speaks.

And then Adler, still looking at the tea, says quietly,
"When I was a boy, I nearly died."

Ram Dass doesn't look surprised.
He simply waits.

Adler continues.
"Rickets. Pneumonia. Weakness in my legs.
I spent more time in bed than I did playing with
other children.
I remember hearing my parents whispering in the
next room,
convinced I wouldn't make it."

He pauses, his voice steady.
"I think that's when I first felt it—
the need to prove I deserved to live.
That I had a place in the world.
I didn't have strength in my body,
so I developed strength in my will."

He lets the words linger,
then takes a breath.

"It made me clever.
But not free."

There's a flicker of something in Ram Dass's
expression—
respect, maybe.
Or brotherhood.

Ram Dass pours the tea into three small ceramic
cups.
He hands one to Adler, then one to me.
The clay is warm in my hands, grounding.
I hold it without drinking.

"My parents didn't think I'd become a teacher," Ram
Dass says,
eyes still on the steam.
"They thought I would disappear into some
intellectual hole and never come out."
He smiles gently.
"They weren't entirely wrong."

"I was raised in comfort.
Education. Privilege.
But it never touched the ache in me.
I climbed ladders without ever asking if they were
leaning against the right wall.
And when I got to the top,
I still felt hollow."

He pauses.

"There was a moment.
I was walking across Harvard Yard.
Successful, young, admired.
But I felt like a ghost.
Like I'd built a life out of mirrors,
and nothing could touch me."

He takes a sip of tea, closes his eyes briefly.

"It wasn't until I met Maharaji
that I saw the mind for what it was.
Brilliant, but limited.
It can get you to the door—
but not through it."

Adler sips his tea.
"And yet, we need the mind to even know there's a door."

Ram Dass grins.
"True.
But it's the heart that walks through."

The room holds that line
like a breath suspended.

∞

I take a sip of my tea.
It's warm. Floral. A bitter finish that lingers like memory.
Suddenly, my chest tightens—
not from the taste,
but from the truth beneath it.
Something in me clenches without permission.

My shoulders curl forward. I shift beneath the blanket.
My fingers tighten around the cup.
Even my breath feels rehearsed—
inhaling for effect,
exhaling just enough to keep the image of calm intact.

I can feel their presence.
Not their judgment.
Their seeing.

They aren't looking at me directly—
but it doesn't matter.
Their attention is everywhere.
In the air.
In the firelight.
In the way silence holds the room
like a parent holds a sobbing child.

I'm not being interrogated.
I'm being revealed.
Not by their words—
but by their willingness to stay.

That's what undoes me.

I flash to college—
2 a.m., alone in the library,
fluorescent lights buzzing overhead,
a stack of psychology and theology books open like
shields.

I remember clenching my jaw so tight
my teeth ached.
Searching for a sentence—any sentence—
that would make me feel okay.

I wasn't studying.
I was hiding.
Trying to build a tower of certainty
tall enough to keep the chaos out.

Ram Dass looks over at Adler,
then back to the fire.

"Sometimes," he says,
"the first identity we create is simply the one that
hurts the least."

The line lands.
Not like insight.
Like recognition.

I don't just hear it.
I feel it.
In the center of my chest,
like a truth I've been dodging
finally stepping into the light.

Adler nods, still watching the flames.
"Or the one that lets us survive the longest."

I swallow hard.
My throat feels raw.
The truth of it is unbearable in its simplicity.

I don't know who I am without the masks.
I don't know if I've ever truly lived without
performance.

I glance down at my hands.
They're trembling slightly—
not enough to be noticed,
unless you're really looking.

I think they're looking.

And somehow,
I don't want to hide.

And yet—
I still do.

A quiet war inside.

I feel it in my chest—
a dense knot of heat and grief and shame.
Like something I've stuffed for decades
has finally started pushing back.

The fire shifts again.
The flames stretch taller, then settle.

I glance toward the window.
The stars are brighter now.
Cold. Infinite.

I want to cry.
And nothing sad has been said.

I want to scream.
Though no one has raised their voice.

I feel like I'm being unraveled by presence.
Dismantled by stillness.

They haven't begun.
But something in me already has.

And it's coming undone
in the softest, most terrifying way imaginable.

∞

I don't know exactly when it happens.

Maybe it's in the flicker of the flame.
Maybe it's in the way Adler gently sets his cup back
on the table.
Maybe it's the way Ram Dass closes his eyes after a
sip—
as if tasting something deeper than tea.

Something shifts.
Not outwardly.
Inwardly.
Like a door that's always been there, quietly opening.

The room is the same.
And yet—it isn't.
The silence now holds a new texture.
Thicker. Softer. Alive.

I feel something ancient stirring beneath my skin.
Not a memory, exactly—
a recognition.
Like I've been here before.
Like my soul remembers this kind of stillness,
even if my mind has no words for it.

There's no music playing,
but I feel rhythm.
No ceremony declared,
but I feel reverence.
No sermon being preached—
but I feel truth.

And then, it dawns on me:

This is sacred.

Not because someone told me it is.
Not because of candles or chants or stained glass.
But because something in me has gone quiet—
and in that quiet, something real has shown up.

Something true began
when I stopped pretending.
When I stopped performing.
When I stopped trying to prove.

It begins when I'm finally still enough to feel.
When I'm brave enough to be seen.
It begins when two people—maybe three—sit in the
firelight
and don't turn away.

I want to cry again.
Not from pain this time.
From awe.

I'm beginning to understand that the real isn't
something I chase.
It's something I recognize when I stop performing.

It's already here.
In the breath I didn't rush.
In the gaze I didn't dodge.
In the memory I let rise.

And now—here I am.

Wrapped in a blanket.
Sitting beside a fire.
Holding a cup of tea,
and feeling—maybe for the first time—
like the moment doesn't need to be anything more.

I don't need to be anything more.

In that stillness, in that surrender—
something sacred begins.

# CHAPTER TWO
## *Becoming Real*

The question comes without warning.
Not in words.
Not from either man.

It rises like smoke—from the silence,
from the firelight,
from the strange safety of being seen.

Who do you think you are?

Not as a challenge.
Not to corner me.
But to invite me into something deeper.
Something truer.

Suddenly, I feel it again.
The grip.
The tension that clings to the version of me I've
worked so hard to make believable.

The curated self.
The competent self.
The spiritual one.
The clever one.
The one who's not too much.

Not too needy.
Not too angry.
Not too lost.

I know how to be that person.
I know how to dress them up.
I've spent years getting them to walk into rooms like
they belong there.

But this isn't a room like those.
Here, that self feels paper-thin.

Ram Dass leans forward slightly and pours another
round of tea.
His eyes never leave the cup,
but I feel the weight of his presence on me
like a hand over my heart.

Adler shifts in his seat. The wood beneath him
creaks.
He doesn't speak.
But something in his gaze says he's watching more
than posture.
He's watching patterns.

I feel exposed again.
But not unsafe.
I wonder—have I ever felt that before?
Exposed, but safe?

My chest tightens.
My breath goes shallow.

My mind reaches for something to say—
something insightful, impressive, distracting.

But I don't speak.
I let the silence stretch.

The fire pops.
The tea steeps.
And I feel the mask begin to itch.

Not physically.
But in my psyche.
Like a tight shirt that suddenly doesn't fit.

A question rises in me, soft and trembling:
If I didn't have to be anyone right now…
who would I be?

The heat in my chest expands.

There's no sermon happening here.
No spotlight.
No performance.

Just two men who keep holding me—
not with arms, but with presence.
And a night that keeps whispering:

You don't have to be who you thought you were.

You can be the one who's breaking.
The one who's remembering.
The one who is not a role—
but a soul.

And maybe…
that is enough.

Maybe that is everything.

∞

No one speaks.

The room holds me.
And slowly, I begin to feel it—

Not a breakdown. Not a meltdown.
But a soft collapse.
A quiet undoing of all the tension I didn't realize I
was still carrying.

My shoulders drop a little.
My jaw unclenches.
Even my spine lets go of its perfect line.

It's as if my body is finally given permission to stop
performing, too.
I didn't expect this.

I didn't expect that being seen
could feel like being exhaled.
But it does.

Ram Dass lifts his cup again, slow and deliberate.
His eyes never rush.
His movements don't ask anything of me.

Adler leans back slightly, and I notice the way his
hands fold gently over one another—

patient, present, almost fatherly.
And suddenly I understand something I've never
had words for:

This is what it feels like to be safe.
Not because nothing hard will happen.
Not because the people in the room will rescue me.
But because no one here is asking me to be anyone
else.

The part of me that always scans, always anticipates,
always tries to match the energy in the room—
begins to go quiet.

It doesn't go away completely.
But it loosens its grip.

And I think of how many years I've spent
armoring myself with humor, insight, humility,
control—
Just to be allowed to stay.
To be enough.
To be safe.
To not be abandoned.

Tears sting the back of my eyes.
Not because I feel broken—
But because I feel whole enough to cry.

No one moves to stop it.
No one rushes to change the moment.

That might be the most sacred thing of all.

My body settles in a way I didn't know it needed to.
The fire crackles once—
like it's exhaling with me.

∞

Ram Dass looks over at Adler and says,
"We spend the first part of life trying to become
someone.
And the second half trying to remember who
we were before we thought we had to become
someone."

Adler hums in agreement, folding his hands
thoughtfully.
Then he speaks.

"And yet we cling to the mask because it's familiar.
We forget that the mask isn't what keeps us safe.
It's what keeps us stuck."

I want to respond.
To say something smart.
Something that proves I belong here.
But I don't.

I just sit there, silently watching the way they look at
each other—
not with analysis,
not even curiosity,
but with something deeper.

Recognition.

Their eyes say what their words don't:

I see your becoming.
I honor what you've had to survive.

And then…
I feel it.

That gaze turns toward me.
Not in unison.
Not with intensity.
Just a shared awareness.
A gentle turning.

Ram Dass's eyes find mine.
And then Adler's.

Slowly. Patiently.

Adler's head tilts slightly.
Ram Dass's hand rests lightly on the table.
No rush.
No invitation to perform.
They just look.

And it is the kindest, most devastating thing I've ever experienced.

Because in that gaze is everything I thought I had to earn.

Respect.
Belonging.
Worth.

They're offering it freely.
Not because I've performed well.
But because I'm here.
Because I'm real.
Because I've stayed.

I feel the tears again,
but they don't fall.

They settle in the corners of my eyes—
like prayers that have found a place to land.

This is what it means
to be held without being fixed.
To be witnessed without being rushed.

And suddenly, I realize—

This is the beginning of becoming real.
Not in their eyes.
In my own.

Not the real that has answers.
The real that still trembles—
but stays anyway.

∞

The fire shifts again.
A log settles into itself.
A small trail of sparks lifts up, curling toward the
chimney—then disappearing.

Outside the windows, the wind presses gently
against the glass—

soft, but present.
Like the world is breathing just beyond the walls.

Ram Dass doesn't speak.
Adler doesn't move.
And somehow, that stillness opens something
deeper than words ever could.

A memory rises.

I'm six—maybe seven—
sitting at the top of the stairs,
listening to my parents argue in the kitchen.

The voices are low, but sharp.
I remember holding my breath
like it might keep the house from falling apart.

That night, I made a choice I didn't know I was
making.

Be good.
Be helpful.
Be quiet.

Make things easier.

They never said those words.
But I heard them.

I heard them in the silence
that followed every slammed cabinet.
I heard them in the way no one checked on me.

I learned to disappear inside of being good.
To shape myself into something that wouldn't add weight.
To become the reason things stayed together—
or at least didn't get worse.

Adler clears his throat softly.

"Most identities aren't chosen," he says.
"They're constructed in the dark—
in the places where love felt most fragile."

I nod before I even realize I'm doing it.

"It doesn't matter how conscious your parents were,"
Ram Dass adds, gently.
"What matters is the meaning you made.
And how you carried that meaning forward—
into school,
into relationships,
into your spirituality."

The tea is still warm in my hands.
And for the first time,
I feel how heavy the cup is.

Not just physically.

It's as if I've been carrying this weight my entire life—

The weight of staying small enough to be safe.
The weight of never being too much.
The weight of being the peacekeeper.

The achiever.
The one who doesn't make things worse.

All of it in the name of love.
All of it in the name of survival.

The room doesn't flinch.
And neither do they.

Ram Dass just refills my cup.

And Adler says quietly,
"We've all been there."

The truth doesn't take the ache away.
But somehow…
it helps me hold it with softer hands.

∞

I carried that survival into everything.

Into classrooms—where I became the one who had
the answers.
Into friendships—where I became the one liked by
everyone.
Into relationships—where I became the person I
thought they wanted.

Into spirituality, too.

I could quote Rumi before I ever let someone see me
cry.
I could hold space for others without ever truly
letting anyone hold space for me.

And for a while—it worked.

People admired me. They leaned on me.
They asked for advice, for insight, for wisdom.

And I gave it.

Not because I didn't care.
But because I didn't know how to stop performing
long enough to ask if I was okay.

The room is quiet again.

Ram Dass has shifted slightly, cross-legged now,
his eyes half-closed like he's listening beyond the
room.

Adler is watching the fire.
His expression unreadable—but soft.

I don't need them to say anything.
Because the air is saying it.
The flames are saying it.

I lived so long trying to become someone who
wouldn't be left.
Someone impressive enough to be loved.
Someone spiritual enough to be safe.

But the truth is—

all of it was armor.
Polished. Beautiful. Believable.
But still…armor.

Adler finally speaks.

"Sometimes the most convincing identity…
is the one built from what worked."

Ram Dass nods.

"Especially if it kept you from feeling what hurt."

I close my eyes.
And I see the truth laid bare:

I've worn the mask of the helper.
The healer.
The good one.
The wise one.

Not because I was false.
But because I was afraid that without the
performance,
there'd be nothing left underneath.

And I wonder—

What if the truth isn't that there's nothing
underneath?
What if it's that I've just never been still long enough
to remember what's there?

Something in me softens.

Not all the way.
But enough to stay.

I open my eyes.

Adler is still watching the fire.
Ram Dass is still breathing like a monk at peace.

And I'm still here.

No one has turned away.

And maybe—just maybe—
I don't have to either.

∞

The silence doesn't feel empty.
It feels precise.
Like the room itself knows what it's doing—

Like it's waiting.
Not impatiently.
Reverently.
For me to meet myself.

Ram Dass sets his cup down. Slowly. Carefully.
The sound of ceramic against wood echoes like a
small bell.

Then he speaks.
Not to provoke—
but to midwife.

"There's a version of you that's done an incredible
job surviving," he says.
"It deserves your gratitude. Not your shame."

I feel my throat tighten.

Adler adds, "The tragedy isn't that we become
someone to be loved.
It's that we forget—it was a strategy."

Their voices don't feel like answers.
They feel like permission.

I shift slightly under the blanket, my fingers
tightening around the mug.
The warmth has seeped into the clay now—deep and
steady.
Like it has in me.

There's a tremble inside I can't name—
Like the quiet before an old door opens.

I'm not being confronted.
I'm being dismantled.

Not with force.
Not with violence.
With presence.

It's that gentleness
that undoes me
more than anything else could have.

Outside, a wind stirs the trees.
I can't see them.
But I hear the hush of their movement—
a soft, ancient murmur,
like the earth itself is bearing witness.

I glance at the two men.

They're not leaning in.
They're not pressing.
They're just here.

And it's in their here-ness
something inside me starts to bend.

My mind tries to hold on—
To make sense.
To reach for words.
To name what's happening.

But my body has already moved ahead.

Something in my chest unspools—
quiet, slow,
and terrifyingly free.

I don't say anything.
But I don't need to.

Something is already speaking through my silence.
And they're listening to that.

∞

The silence has changed.
It's no longer holding me.
It's inviting me.

Like the center of a circle—
quietly waiting to be stepped into.

But I don't want to speak just to fill the space.
I've done that before.
Too many times.

Given answers before questions had even finished
forming.
Offered wisdom before sitting with truth.
Told stories that made pain sound poetic—
just so I wouldn't have to feel the ache.

I look down at my hands.
They're steady now.
But my chest is tight—
like something is knocking from the inside.

I inhale slowly.
The air smells like cedar and fire.
Earth and warmth.

Safe enough.

And so I speak.

Not loud.
Not brave.
Just…real.

My fingers curl tighter around the mug.
The heat grounds me.
I close my eyes for half a second—
and I let it come.

"I don't know who I am if I'm not performing."

Ram Dass doesn't move.
Adler doesn't blink.
They let the words land like soft rain.

I swallow.
"I don't know how to be loved without doing
something to earn it.
And I think…"
"I think I've spent most of my life terrified that if I
stopped being impressive, I'd be forgotten."

There it is.
The thing I never say.

Not because I'm hiding it.
But because I've lived so long inside it,
I forgot it was something I could name.

The fire crackles again—
gentle, like a breath releasing tension.

Adler's eyes soften. "That's not weakness," he says.
"That's awareness."

Ram Dass nods slowly. "And it's the beginning of
love."

My throat closes again—
but not from fear.
From the rawness of being received.

Not fixed.
Not redirected.
Just…met.

I don't say anything else.
I don't need to.

Because something in me knows—

That was the first real confession.
And no one turned away.

∞

I don't mean to go back there,
but something opens—
and the memory rushes in.

Uninvited.
But welcome.

I was thirteen. A Friday night at the movies.
The kind of night that smelled like buttered popcorn
and Axe body spray—
thick in the air, like everyone was trying just a little
too hard.

Our parents had dropped us off, and for a moment,
we felt grown.

Loose bills in our pockets.
Soda lids popping.
Neon lights buzzing above us like we belonged
somewhere.

I don't remember the movie.
Not the plot. Not the punchlines.

But I remember the moment I laughed—
too loud, too sharp,
like it was part of a script
I didn't know I'd been handed.

It wasn't funny.
But I laughed anyway.
Because that's what everyone else was doing.

Silence would have meant standing out.
And standing out felt like death.

So I scanned the faces around me,
looking for proof that I was doing it right—
a nod, a grin, any kind of signal
that I wasn't alone in my pretending.

I needed that
more than oxygen.
More than truth.
More than myself.

And in that moment,
I began to disappear.

Not all at once—
but like a slow dissolve, frame by frame.

Like that scene in *Back to the Future*
where the photograph fades—
my smile still holding,
but my soul slipping quietly out of frame.

The boy in the picture still looked alive.
But something essential had already left.

I didn't know it then.
But I was rehearsing something
I would perfect in the years to come:

Becoming whoever the moment needed me to be.
Shrinking in just the right way to earn belonging.
Laughing in just the right tone to stay safe.

It's wild how early the performance begins—
and how long we forget it's a role.

I was becoming a projection.
An echo of what others wanted.
And I didn't know the word for it then.

But I know it now:
Grief.

Not for what was done to me—
but for who I never got to be.

I see him now.
Thirteen.
Trying so hard to belong.
Still wearing the laugh like armor.

And I don't try to change him.
I just sit beside him.

Inside the frame of that fading photograph.

Not as someone who's fixed—
but as someone who remembers.

Ram Dass hasn't spoken.
Adler hasn't moved.
But I feel them with me.

That's what makes the memory safe enough to stay
with.

I keep my eyes open this time.
Let it play.
Let it ache.

And I don't try to fix it.
I just breathe.

And in that breath—something cracks.

Not with sound.
Not with drama.
But with relief.

And for the first time,
I think—

Maybe that old version of me
doesn't have to be buried.

Maybe he's not dead.
Maybe he's just been waiting
for me to come back for him.

And maybe, for the first time,
I'm the one who stays with him.

Not to rescue—
just to remember.

∞

The room doesn't change.
But something in me does.

Not all at once—
just enough to notice.

Like the difference between holding your breath…
and realizing you don't have to anymore.

The fire cracks softly.
A log collapses inward, and I feel it mirror the shift
happening in me—
not a falling apart,
but a falling in.

A return.

I don't say anything.
Neither do they.

Ram Dass just offers me a slight smile—
the kind that holds lifetimes in it.

Adler doesn't move.
His eyes are closed, but somehow,
I know he's listening with his whole being.

I sit with it.
With him.
With me.

And it's quiet—
in the best way.

For so long, I thought the work was about becoming
someone new.
But maybe...
it's more about remembering who I was
before the performance began.

Before the masks.
Before the roles.
Before the ache of invisibility
taught me to vanish myself.

I can feel something now.
A kind of rootedness.
Not in answers—
but in presence.

Not in confidence—
but in truth.

And maybe...
that's enough.

Maybe the shift isn't always seismic at all.
Maybe it's just the softest decision—

To stay with yourself
when it would be easier to vanish.

# CHAPTER THREE
## *The Cost of Becoming*

The fire has settled into a soft, steady rhythm.

Its light no longer flickers like an invitation—

It glows now, familiar.

Like it's settled in for the long night ahead.

Like it knows it will be needed.

Outside, the night deepens, pressing against the windows like a velvet wave. Inside, the warmth is almost deceptive. It wraps around us like safety, but I can feel the next wave coming—the part of the night where the masks are no longer enough to keep me from drowning.

The room doesn't move.
But something in it waits—
not impatiently,
but like it knows what's coming.

Adler speaks first.

This time, his voice is low, steady. The kind of voice that doesn't raise questions, but raises memories.

"There's a moment in every person's life when striving stops feeling noble and starts feeling heavy."

Ram Dass nods, his cup resting loosely in his fingers. "The illusion of becoming something is intoxicating," he says.

"Until it isn't."

∞

Adler leans forward slightly.
His voice is gentle, but clear—
like he's not trying to teach me something,
but name something I already know.

"In my practice," he says, "I often saw people carrying unspoken contracts from childhood.

'If I succeed…I'll be safe.'
'If I'm impressive…I'll be loved.'
'If I don't need anything…I won't be a burden.'"

He pauses. Not for effect, but to let the weight of those words settle into the room.

Then, quieter—
"These beliefs aren't written. They're absorbed. And they shape our entire trajectory."

Ram Dass lifts his eyes from the fire.
"It's a kind of spiritual amnesia," he says.

"We forget who we are—and start building a self
that will win us approval, success, security."

He pauses too.
Not because he's uncertain—
but because something sacred is stirring.

"We build and build…but we never feel whole."

The silence that follows is deeper than before.
Not heavy. Just *honest*.

My jaw tightens.
I shift beneath the blanket.
And then—
a memory rises.

Middle school.
A driveway, holding a basketball.
My friend, casually asks if he can take my crush out
on a date.

"Of course," I say too quickly.
I laugh it off, like it doesn't sting.
Like it doesn't matter.

Inside, something hardens.

A quiet voice begins to form—
not loud enough to notice then,
but strong enough to shape me for years.

Don't show too much.
Don't feel too much.

Be easy to like.
Be impossible to hurt.

I've lived in service to that voice.
I shaped myself around it,
without ever realizing I was kneeling to a belief.

A contract I never signed.
But obeyed all the same.

No one says a word.
But I can feel the others are with me.
Not interpreting. Just staying.

And somehow, that makes the memory safe enough
to feel.

∞

Ram Dass turns toward me. His eyes are soft, not
searching—
just present, like he's waiting for a door to open on
its own.

"What were you rewarded for?" he asks.
The question hangs there.
Not a challenge.
Just an offering.

I don't answer right away. My hand tightens around
the mug, feeling the heat.
I search for the right words—but what comes up is a
feeling, not a sentence.

"Being good," I say at last.
"Being strong. Not complaining. Winning."

Adler tilts his head, studying the light in the hearth,
not me.
And then—
The line that doesn't rush,
That doesn't blink—
But drops like a weighty stone:

"And what did that cost you?"

The question doesn't echo.
It expands.
It deepens.

I hesitate, the answer catching at the edge of my
breath.
My throat tightens.

"I don't know. Intimacy, maybe. Vulnerability. I
had friends, but…I always felt like I was outside of
something."

Ram Dass nods slowly.
"That's the shadow of performance," Ram Dass says
softly.
Even when people love you…"

He pauses. Not for drama—
But to let the ache arrive.

"…it doesn't land."

Another pause.

"Because they're loving the version you're showing them—
Not the one you've hidden."

The room goes still
And something in me breaks open—not in pain,
But in truth.
Because I know exactly what that feels like.

The only sound is the fire shifting, the slow exhale of burning wood. A memory comes, slow and heavy. High school baseball. Bottom of the last inning. I get the game-winning hit.

The crowd erupts.
For a moment, I'm weightless—
my dad's arms wrapped around me, the field beneath my cleats,
the night air electric with approval.

But later, alone in bed,
The cheers echo in my ears.
Then fade.
And what's left…is silence.

All that's left is the hollow ache inside. I thought that moment would fix everything.

It didn't.

The fire groans beside me,
as if it remembers too—
the ache of applause that doesn't heal.

Another memory rises—my friend's wedding.

I'm in the photos, smiling, toasting, laughing on cue.
But I remember watching him with his bride—
how he let her see him,
and feeling an ache I couldn't name.
I couldn't remember the last time I'd let someone
look at me like that.
Really see me.

I had mastered the art of revealing just enough—
maybe eighty percent—and hiding the rest beneath
charm, competence, and control.

The softest parts stayed hidden. I couldn't risk
rejection.

I had an image to uphold.
A role to perform.
Love to earn.

No one rushes me.
Adler and Ram Dass let the silence stretch—
as if the room itself knows
how long these truths have waited to be spoken.

For a long moment, I just breathe.

Not performing.
Not winning.
Not acting.

Just breathing—and letting the roles I've played finally speak for themselves. And for the first time, I don't interrupt them.

∞

The fire shifts again—soft and deliberate. A log settles into itself, exhaling a breath of smoke into the air above.

Adler leans forward slightly. His voice is quiet, but it lands like truth wrapped in silk.

"There's a moment when ambition stops being a vehicle for growth," he says, "and becomes a hiding place."

Ram Dass chuckles softly—not dismissively, but knowingly. "Yes. And the ego is brilliant at disguising hiding as heroism."

I laugh, too.

But it catches in my throat.

It's not the light kind of laugh—the freeing kind. It's the kind that's laced with recognition.

The kind you use when something hits too close to home and you're not ready to cry.

Ram Dass notices. He always notices. His expression softens, and when he speaks again, it's not to instruct—it's to soothe.

"It's okay," he says. "It's how we all survive at first. But eventually, the cost becomes too great."

The flames crackle again. Outside, the wind presses gently against the windows—like the world is leaning in to listen.

Adler's voice joins again, steady and certain. "And often, we keep striving not because we love what we're chasing—but because we're afraid of what will surface if we stop."

The words don't land in my mind.

They land in my body.

Like a stone in the gut. Like truth in the chest. Like something I've known forever but never dared say aloud.

I swallow.
There's a silence inside me now—not empty, but full.
"I think…"
I pause, my eyes fixed on the shadows dancing across the floor.

"If I stop achieving, I don't know what's left of me."

Ram Dass meets my eyes, and he doesn't look away—not for a moment.

His voice doesn't rise.
It steadies.

And what he says—

Doesn't just land.
It *undoes*.
"But it's a lie. What's beneath is your being. And it's never been not enough."

The room holds still.

Not as a pause,
As a presence.

And in that presence, something older than memory begins to melt.
Not just in me.

But in you, too.

Because we've all carried this secret.
The one that says: *If I stop becoming, I'll disappear.*

But here, in this room, beside this fire, in the presence of two men who see what's real—

That secret doesn't need to be carried anymore.
It doesn't need to be solved or silenced.
It just needs to be felt.
Held in the light.
And then, maybe…released.

∞

Adler turns to me again, his tone slower now. More tender.

"Do you remember when you first felt like you had to prove yourself?"

The question doesn't surprise me. But the ache it touches does.

I nod, eyes fixed somewhere between the floor and the fire.

"Yeah," I say quietly. "Puberty hit hard. I felt lost in my own body. Insecure. Like I was supposed to be something I didn't understand."

Ram Dass doesn't speak. He simply *waits*—not for an answer, but for something to open. His silence stretches wide, like a hand gently holding the space.

I keep going.

"I didn't feel man enough. Whatever that meant. So I copied what I saw—toughness, detachment. I joined teams. I made jokes. I flirted. I studied how to belong. But underneath…"

I pause, the words catching on something deep and unspoken.

"…underneath, I felt like I was faking it."

Adler nods, his voice soft. "That's the beginning of disconnection. From the self. From the body. From authentic desire."

I nod, too. Slowly.

"I buried so much. The confusion about sex. The shame about not knowing what I wanted. Or who. I didn't feel safe enough to ask the questions. So I performed instead."

The fire snaps—sharp and small, like punctuation.

Ram Dass finally speaks. Not with correction. With reverence.

"And yet," he says, "all of it was sacred. Even the confusion."
He pauses.
"Especially the confusion."

I turn to look at him.

He's not performing that sentence.
He *believes* it.

And that's what undoes me.

Because if he believes that, then maybe I don't have to hate the part of me that wandered.
Maybe I don't have to hide the younger version of me that didn't know who he was, only who he was supposed to be.

Maybe even that version is worth loving.

∞

The fire pops again—soft, like a breath releasing tension.

Adler lifts his cup and takes a slow sip of tea.

"You've mentioned your father," he says carefully, voice low and steady. "What was his love like?"

I stare into the flames.

The question isn't harsh. But it stirs something tender.

"He is a good man. Truly.
He worked hard. He showed up. He gave me more than he ever received.
In many ways, I can't imagine having a better father."

And yet...

I feel a familiar ache rise in my throat. The one I've swallowed a hundred times before.

"He wanted the world for me," I say slowly. "And he gave it. With his actions. His commitment. His strength."

I pause. My voice softens.

"But for some reason…his love still felt 'earned.' Not freely available."

The words hang in the air like smoke.

Adler nods. "And so, the striving began."

I blink back the burn behind my eyes. Not from pain. From recognition.

Ram Dass speaks gently, like someone holding something fragile in his hands.

"When love is earned," he says, "the soul contracts. It learns to perform, to please, to adapt. But the soul was never meant to bend that way."

His words land like a truth I already knew, but never dared name.

My jaw tightens.

I swallow.

"Sometimes," I say, "I wonder if I ever really allowed myself to know what unconditional love felt like."

Adler leans forward just slightly. "And yet," he says with quiet certainty, "you're here. Which means some part of you never gave up hoping for it."

I don't respond right away.

The tea warms my hands. My breath deepens.

And suddenly, the tears arrive—not in panic, not in grief.

In relief.

Something in me wants to weep—not because I'm
sad, but because I've never said this out loud:

"I'm tired of becoming," I whisper.
The words feel ancient.
Like they've been waiting for decades.
"I just want to be."

The room holds its breath.
No one rushes to answer.
Because they know—
This is not a statement.
It's a surrender.

I think I spent years impressing people who
reminded me of him—
Bosses.
Mentors.
Even spiritual teachers.
Hoping that one of them would finally say:

*You don't have to do anything else.*

But none of them ever did.
Because that voice isn't out there.

It's in here.

That's the moment the chase ends.
When the seeker stops running.
And finally listens to the voice that was never
missing—
Only quiet.

The room doesn't react.

It receives.

And I realize—I may have spent my whole life chasing a smile.

But here, in this stillness, I'm learning how to return to myself instead.

∞

Ram Dass closes his eyes briefly, like he's listening inward before he speaks.

"You don't have to earn your way into being," he says softly.

The words land like a hand on my chest.

Adler's voice follows, low and steady. "And you don't have to prove yourself worthy of rest."

Something in me exhales.

Not my breath.
Something older.
Something that's been clenched for years—maybe decades.

I don't respond right away.

I just feel it.
That version of me—the one who performed, who impressed, who ran faster than his own

exhaustion—he's still here.
But he's not driving anymore.

I speak—quiet, honest.

"I've been living for applause that doesn't heal me."
The fire doesn't crackle. The silence doesn't push back.
They just listen.

.

"And chasing love in places that were never safe."

Ram Dass's eyes find mine. They're not searching.
They're seeing.

"You can forgive that version of yourself," he says.
"He was just doing his best."

I nod, but it's more than agreement.

It's a loosening.

Because he's right.

That younger self—the achiever, the pleaser, the performer—
he was never bad.

He was just scared. And trying. And tired.

And maybe…
he deserves more than analysis.
More than reframes.
More than strategy.

Maybe…he deserves compassion.
Not as a technique.
As a homecoming.

No one says anything else.

The fire crackles quietly—lower now, more glow than flame.
The room feels like it's breathing with me.

I don't need to fix anything.

I don't need to explain anything.

And for the first time tonight…

I let the silence hold me.

And it does.

∞

The fire has softened into a quiet bed of coals—steady, low, glowing.

Ram Dass reaches for the firewood and adds a fresh log. He doesn't speak, doesn't hurry. The log settles in with a sigh of smoke.

Adler pours another round of tea. His movements are simple. Careful. Ceremonial.

No one says anything profound.

They don't need to.

Because right now, the stillness between us is the teaching.

The warmth in the room is more than heat. It's memory. It's presence. It's the kind of silence that doesn't demand anything from you—but still rearranges you from the inside out.

I look at the window.

Beyond it, the stars shimmer in silence.
Still there.
Still watching.
Still waiting.

Something in me whispers—
not a thought,
not a mantra,
something *older* than that.

*You are not here to become.*
*You are here to return.*

Return to the you beneath the striving.
Beneath the noise.
Beneath the shape you learned to take to be loved.

You are not here to become.
You are here to remember.

And the path back…
Is not grand.
It's not impressive.

It's breath by breath.
Layer by layer.
A quiet surrender to the truth that never stopped
waiting for you.
And so, I do.

Not all at once.
Not with fanfare.

Just one breath at a time.
One layer at a time.
One quiet surrender at a time.

# CHAPTER FOUR
## *The Tender Threshold*

The fire's light flickers along the stone walls, casting shadows that seem to move with their own breath.

The warmth is still here.

But it feels different now.

Like it's not just heating the room—
It's loosening something inside me.
A thaw.

No one speaks.

For a long time.

And the silence isn't uncomfortable.
It's sacred.
Like something fragile has been laid between us,
and no one dares speak too loudly for fear it might shatter.

I sip my tea slowly, holding it with both hands now.

The cup is warm against my palms.
Grounding.

The steam curls upward in slow spirals, catching the light before dissolving into nothing.

Everything tonight has felt slow.
Precise.
Like some invisible rhythm is guiding the way—one I didn't create but am somehow moving to.

This isn't a wound being ripped open.

It's a bandage coming loose.

Gently.

Revealing something I'd almost forgotten was there.

Ram Dass stirs—just a shift in posture, but it feels intentional. Like a bell being rung without sound.

"You're very brave," he says softly.

I blink. "Why?"

He gestures toward me—his hand moving not outward, but inward. Toward my chest. Toward my core.

"Because you're staying," he says. "Even though part of you is already trying to run."

The words land.

Not sharply.

But deeply.

I nod, my eyes fixed on the fire. The flames blur slightly, and I realize I haven't blinked in a while.

"It's loud in my head right now," I whisper.

Adler's voice enters the space like a balm.

"What's it saying?"

I hesitate.

And in the hesitation, I feel it.

That tight swirl in my gut.
The flutter in my chest.
The old, quiet panic beneath the surface.

"It's saying I've said too much," I answer.
"That I'm too exposed.
That this isn't safe."

Ram Dass's smile is soft—not dismissive, not trying to reassure. Just presence.

"That voice is trying to protect you," he says.
"But it's also what's kept you separate for a very long time."

His words don't land with weight.

They land with warmth.

And I sit there, between the fire and the men and the silence and my own trembling body—

Knowing they're right.

And unsure if I'm ready to stop running.

But still…
Here.

∞

Adler leans forward, his voice as gentle as the worn blanket folded neatly on my chair—familiar, unassuming, and quietly warm.

"What's the cost of staying armored?"

The question doesn't pierce.
It doesn't need to.

It lands.

Heavy. Honest.
Like a stone placed in the center of the room.

I don't answer.

Not right away.

Because something in me already knows.

And it hurts.

I close my eyes.

The fire crackles softly beside me—warm, steady, alive. I feel the clay of the cup in my hands. My palms are sweating now. My breath has gone shallow.

And then—there it is.

A memory I rarely touch.

I'm in my early twenties, standing in a crowded room at a party.
Music is loud. Lights dim. Everyone is laughing, flirting, drinking.
I'm on. I'm clever. I'm charming. I know exactly what to say.
I make people laugh—the kind of laugh that makes you feel powerful. Wanted.
They look at me like I matter.

I leave late that night, buzzing.
The adrenaline of attention still humming in my skin.
But when I get home…

It's silent.

I lie awake in bed, staring at the ceiling.

And suddenly, all the light drains out of me.

The laughter doesn't echo.
The compliments don't stick.
The cleverness feels like a costume I forgot to take off.

And I feel…
hollow.

Used.
Not by them.
By myself.

Like I rented my body out for approval and forgot to ask what it needed in return.

I wasn't just tired.

I was empty.

I take a slow, shaky breath.

My eyes are still closed.

"The cost," I whisper, "Connection. Real connection."

The room doesn't move.
Doesn't rush to respond.

Adler nods slowly, his eyes soft.

Ram Dass adds quietly, "And without connection, there's no nourishment for the soul. We starve— even if the world thinks we're thriving."

His words settle like ash on the surface of the tea.

I open my eyes.
Look into the fire.

And then I say it.

Not for impact.
Not for drama.
Just because it's true.

"I've been starving in plain sight."

The words fall into the room like a dropped bowl.
They don't shatter.
They echo.

And they see me.
Not the charming version.
Not the clever one.
Just…me.
And they don't look away.

*Maybe you know what that's like.*
*To be applauded, but untouched.*
*To wonder if anyone has ever actually loved you—not*
*the mask, but the marrow.*

∞

Ram Dass looks at me again with that unbearable
kindness—the kind that doesn't try to rescue, the
kind that stays steady while your insides shake.

"Shame is sticky," he says softly.
"It doesn't always scream. Sometimes it just
whispers, *'Don't let them see this part of you.'*"

His voice doesn't carry judgment.

Only understanding.

Adler speaks next, folding his hands in his lap. "And so we bury it. We build whole personalities on top of it. Achievers. Helpers. Jokers. Lovers. Teachers."

His eyes don't flinch when he says it.

He's naming masks we've all worn.

I let out a laugh—but it's sharp. Dry. Bitter.

"All my greatest strengths," I say, "have been cover-ups."

They don't contradict me.

They don't reach for a reframe.
They don't hand me a compliment to soften the blow.

And that's what makes this space different.

No one here is trying to fix me.

They're just staying.

And in that staying, I feel something I hadn't expected:

Not safety. Not yet.

Exposure.

A mirror is being held up.

And in it, I don't see the clever one.
The strong one.
The wise one.

I see the one who's spent a lifetime performing lovability.

And now…

I'm face-to-face with the fear that who I really am—beneath the charm, beneath the insight, beneath the polish—might not be enough.

The silence between us stretches, but it doesn't feel empty.
It feels like it's waiting for the truth.

Ram Dass watches me, and his voice comes like a hand on the shoulder.

"Have you ever shown someone your pain," he asks, "and been met with love instead of distance?"

I pause.

I want to say yes.

A few flickers come to mind—brief moments.
A late-night conversation.
A quiet hug that lingered too long.

But if I'm honest?

In truth…

"I've rarely given anyone the opportunity," I say.

"To see my pain.
And love me in it."

I take a breath.
An then I say the thing I've never said—not out loud. Not to anyone.

I pause.

"I don't trust it," I admit.
My voice is low. Bare.
"Not love.
Not yet.
Not when it comes without a price."

Adler doesn't flinch.

But he doesn't let it slide either.

He studies me for a long beat. Then says, "That's a beautiful line."

I blink, thrown off.

"'Not when it comes without a price,'" he repeats.
"That's poetry. It's sharp. Polished. Insightful."

I nod slightly, unsure if it's a compliment.

"But I wonder," he adds—soft, but surgical—"do you believe it?"

I stiffen.

He's not being cruel. Not even unkind.

But the room shifts.

Something in his voice catches on a thread I didn't know was hanging loose. And suddenly I feel it all unraveling.

He continues, "You've been incredibly articulate tonight. Honest, even. But there's a difference between speaking the truth and *living* it."

He tilts his head slightly, eyes unwavering.

"And sometimes the most elegant confessions are just rehearsed ways of staying hidden."

It doesn't hit like a slap. It hits like being *seen*—too clearly, too deeply.

Ram Dass doesn't say anything.

That absence—his silence—slices sharper than words.

The warmth in the room shifts.

The fire flickers lower.
A breeze slips through a crack in the window.
I feel the chill snake around my ankles.
The closeness I'd felt only moments ago evaporates.

I feel exposed.
Not in a sacred, holy way.
In a *naked and ashamed* way.

Like I've been trying to belong—and they just realized I'm an imposter.

Like they're letting me sit here out of pity.

Something twists in my gut.

I shift in my chair, trying to keep my face still. My shoulders pull in slightly, almost imperceptibly. A reflex. A shield.

I offer a half-smile, like I'm trying to meet Adler halfway. Lighten it. Play the good participant.

"I mean…I've shared a lot tonight," I say, softly. "I'm being honest, I think."

He doesn't respond.

That's when I feel it—
A flicker of discomfort. Not quite fear. Not quite sadness.
Something subtler. Slimier.

Like I've just said something stupid and didn't realize it until the words were already out.
Like I've been trying so hard to be real, and I still got it wrong.
Like I'm being watched—but not seen.

My throat closes a little. I glance at Ram Dass. He's watching me with those wide, ocean eyes. I look away fast.

Something twists in my stomach.

They know.

That's the voice that rises inside—familiar, quiet, cruel.

They know you're a fraud.
They know this is all performance.
They're just too kind to say it out loud.

I try to sit taller, but I feel small.
I try to smile again, but it feels like a lie.

I don't even know what I said wrong.
I just feel…wrong.

Ashamed.
But I don't know it's shame yet.

It shows up first as disorientation.
Then self-hatred.
Then heat in the chest.
Then the slow realization that I'd give anything to disappear.

Adler leans forward, voice low. No edge.

"You're still performing," he says.

I swallow hard.

"You're being honest enough to pass for vulnerable," he continues. "But the moment something stings, you retreat. You tell us how you *used to* be. You keep it tidy. But you're not here yet. Not fully."

I want to defend myself.
I want to explain that this is just how I talk. That I *am* trying.

And then something else surges up—*anger*.

A flash of it. A spike.
Toward Adler. Toward both of them.
How dare they assume this isn't real for me?

They don't know what it's cost me to even be here.

But even as that thought fires through me, another voice rises—smoother, sweeter, more manipulative.

Win him back.

My gaze drifts to Ram Dass again. I want him to smile. To step in. To rescue me from this moment.

I want to *be good* again.
To impress him.
To show him I can take the hit and still look holy.

The performative self kicks in—high gear.
Telling me to find the right words, say something soulful, recover the image.

And that's when it hits.
The exposure.

The drop in my stomach.
The shame.

It doesn't scream.
It whispers.

They see it.
The neediness.
The not-enoughness.
The mask trying so hard to be transparent.

I can't breathe right.
My chest tightens.
My arms feel foreign.
My fingers start to tingle.
Everything in me says: *Hide.*

"I—I need some air," I mutter, already rising.

The room blurs slightly. I feel my body, but I'm not in it. I'm hovering above, watching myself stumble toward the door.

Ram Dass's voice cuts through the silence, soft as smoke:

"It's okay to leave.
Just make sure the one who's walking away isn't the one who's finally ready to be seen."

I stop.

The room steadies.

I turn back, slowly, and lower myself back into the chair.

Still shaking. Still ashamed.
But I stay.

∞

I don't speak for a while.

No one does.

The room is still, but it's changed.
Not just in temperature—though the fire has dimmed and the air feels cooler on my skin now.
It's the kind of stillness that comes after something honest has torn through the air.
Like the soul is slowly reassembling itself after a small death.

My body feels far away—like it belongs to someone else.
But I'm in it.
Barely.
Shaking, yes. But present.

The silence doesn't press.
It holds.

And slowly…
I feel the chair beneath me again.
The mug in my hands.
The faint crackle of the fire as another log settles.

I don't know what they see in me now.
But no one has moved.

They haven't looked away.

And neither do I.

Something shifts in my chest.
Not a release—
a pressure.

A swelling behind the ribs. Tight. Familiar. Hollow.
I want to cry.
God, I want to.
But the tears won't come.
Instead, I feel…nothing.
Not peace. Not presence.
Just the blank weight of numbness.

Ram Dass sees it. Of course, he does.
"Sometimes the tears don't arrive," he says gently,
"because we've dammed the river for too long."
His words don't push.
They wait.

Adler nods, hands folded.
"The body needs to feel safe," he says, "before it will
let go."

I nod—barely.
"I'm trying," I whisper.
"But there's so much locked inside.
I've sat in rooms full of people who loved me—
and still felt like a ghost."

The sentence falls like a stone.
No one tries to lift it.

My shoulders are high, like I've been bracing for a
blow that never came.
My chest is full, not with breath—
with things I never said.

Ram Dass leans forward slightly—
a quiet bow toward something sacred.
"Then don't force it," he says.
"Just sit with the one who is trying.
He's enough."

Something in me softens.
Not all of me.
Just the edge.

My throat tightens.
My eyes sting.
The ache doesn't rush in.
It comes in waves—
small ones.

Grief for the years I kept people out.
For the smiles that masked the dying inside.
For the love I never let in.

And then—
a single tear.
Slow. Hot.

I don't wipe it away.
The fire cracks beside me.
The night breathes through the window.

And I'm still here.
Less ghost.
More human.

∞

Ram Dass leans forward, careful and slow, and gently stirs the embers with an iron poker.

Sparks rise—soft, orange, weightless.

Like tiny stars.

Each one flickering out before it finds a place to land.

"You know," he says quietly, "the armor doesn't just protect us."

He pauses, watching the fire.

"It isolates us.
It keeps out love while pretending to keep out harm."

The words settle in the air.

They don't stab.
They ache.

I feel them in my chest—tight, full, trembling beneath the ribs.

A quiet pressure behind the eyes.
The familiar hum of holding back.

Only this time, I don't.

Not entirely.

A tear had already escaped earlier—
But now, more come.

Not in a flood.
In slow surrender.

I turn slightly away, instinctively.
The old reflex kicks in: *Don't let them see.*

But they don't look away.

Adler watches me with the same stillness as before—
a silence that doesn't retreat, doesn't tighten.

"You're allowed to be tired," he says.

His words touch deeper than the ache.

"You've been carrying the weight of proving your
worth," he continues,
"for a very long time."

I nod, slowly, breath hitching in my throat.

It's not the first tear.

It's the first time I've cried in front of someone
and not felt ashamed.

Ram Dass doesn't speak to soothe me.

He just nods, gently.

"There it is," he says.
"The holy breaking."

His words don't fix anything.

They witness it.

"The shell that never fit you is cracking," he says.
"Let it."

The fire pops beside me—soft and sure.

And for a long while—
no one speaks.

We just sit.

In the warmth.
In the silence.
In the unraveling.

And something begins to move inside me.

Not forward. Not upward.

Downward.

Into a deeper place.

Not pain. But what pain had always covered.

And from that place, I hear it again—
not a thought,
but a remembering.

You are not here to be perfect.
You are here to be whole.

And this breaking?

It's not the end.

It's the door.

∞

Adler's voice is low, steady. Like he's not just
speaking to me—but to something *inside* me.

"We all create stories to survive," he says.
"But at some point, those stories become cages."

The words land heavy.
Not like blame.

Like truth.

Ram Dass adds softly, "The ego doesn't want to die.
It wants to stay in control.
Even if that means keeping you small."

I don't respond right away.

I take a slow sip of tea.
The cup is warm. My hands are not.

"My story has always been…"
I pause. The words taste old.
Like something I've rehearsed so many times I
forgot it was a performance.

"Be useful. Be easy. Be strong—
and people will love you."

I exhale deeply after hearing the words said aloud.

The fire hums beside me.

Adler tilts his head, not unkindly.

"And have they?" he asks.

I look down.

Swallow.

"Yeah," I say.
"They've loved the version of me I gave them."

Ram Dass nods, eyes soft with knowing.

"That's the heartbreak, isn't it?" he says.
"To be surrounded by love…
but feel unseen."

The lump rises in my throat again.

But I don't fight it this time.

I nod—barely.

"I've never let myself be fully seen," I say.
"Not really.
I didn't think I could survive it."

Adler leans back, his presence still close.
His voice is quieter now. As if he's speaking to the part of me that still isn't sure.

"What if surviving," he asks,
"isn't the goal anymore?"

The words don't rush me.

They *hollow me.*

The room is still.

Even the fire seems to lean in.

And in that stillness, I feel it—
not grief for what was done to me.

But grief for what I gave up in order to be loved.

And the quiet, sacred question:

What would it mean to be loved…
without performing for it?

∞

Ram Dass turns toward me, his voice low and steady.

"You're already enough," he says.
"Just as you are.

Not the mask.
Not the performance.
You."

The words don't land how they're supposed to.

They don't spark confidence.
They don't crack me open.
If anything…they make something tighten in my chest.

Because how could he know that?
He doesn't know the things I've done.
He doesn't know the parts I'm still hiding—even here, even now.

A flicker of defensiveness rises.
Not because I want to argue.
But because I want it to be true.
And I don't know how to let it be.

Ram Dass doesn't pull away.
He doesn't try to convince me.

He just stays quiet.

Adler doesn't add anything.
No insight. No diagnosis.
Just the firelight dancing in the silence.

And in that silence…

Something softens.

Not belief. Not yet.

But maybe…

Maybe it doesn't have to be true for me to stay.

Maybe staying *is* the beginning of it becoming true.

Adler's voice enters the stillness.

"You don't have to arrive at wholeness tonight," he
says softly.
"Just stay present to what's falling apart."

The fire has shifted again.
The glow is no longer sharp.
It's golden now. Gentle.

Outside, the night deepens.

And for the first time in longer than I can
remember…
I'm not trying to be anything.
Not curating.
Not proving.
Not fixing.

I'm just…here.

In this room.
With these two men.
And the version of myself I've been hiding from
for years.

He's here too.

He's not healed.
Not whole.

But he's breathing.

And he's staying.

And maybe, just maybe…
Staying is how the soul begins to return.

# CHAPTER FIVE

## *Into the Mystery*

The fire is low now, mostly embers.
The room feels heavier.
Not oppressive—just full.

As if every truth that's been spoken tonight is still
hovering in the air,
curling like smoke around us,
refusing to leave.

Outside, the sky has gone indigo black.
Midnight is close.
The halfway point.
The dying of the old self.

There's something sacred about the silence here.
Like we've entered a chapel not built by hands,
but by presence.

Ram Dass leans back in his chair and exhales
through his nose,
like someone who's just let go of something
he didn't realize he was holding.

He watches the fire—long enough for it to feel like a prayer—
before speaking.

"You know what's funny?" he says, his voice low, almost amused.
"I used to think surrender was a kind of spiritual failure.
Like I'd tried everything else and couldn't hack it, so I just gave up."

Adler smirks without looking up.
"Ah, the ego hates giving up.
It much prefers phrases like '*strategic pivot*' or '*graceful recalibration.*'"

Ram Dass chuckles.
"Exactly. 'Surrender' felt like admitting weakness.
But really, it was the first honest thing I ever did."

A pause.

Not awkward. Just full.

I glance between them, then into the fire.
A part of me wants to say something profound.
Another part wants to disappear into the stillness.

"What changed?" I ask, almost surprising myself with the question.

Ram Dass shrugs,
but the shrug feels old—like the shedding of a layer he no longer needs.

"I got tired of holding on," he says.
"To my image. My intellect. My control.
It wasn't working.
And the deeper truth was—none of it had ever really
been mine."

The fire shifts, letting out a soft pop.

Adler nods, finally lifting his gaze.
"Control is the ultimate illusion," he says.
"But it's a seductive one.
Especially for those of us who were never allowed to
feel safe in chaos."

A silence settles again—
not empty,
but reverent.

As if the room itself is listening.

∞

Ram Dass refills our cups, careful and quiet.
He moves slowly, reverently—like the tea itself is
part of the teaching.
The scent is different now.
Deeper.
Earthier.
I wonder if it's a new blend…
or if I've simply changed how I receive it.

I hold the cup close,
letting the warmth seep into my hands before I sip.

Adler watches the steam rise, then lifts the cup to his lips.
He doesn't rush.

"The desire to control is rooted in fear," he says softly.
"But most of us learned to call it responsibility."

The sentence doesn't sting.
It *unmasks*.

He turns toward me.
His eyes are kind—too kind for the question he asks next.

"What do you fear will happen if you let go?"

I don't answer.

Not right away.

The fire hums beside us.
The tea warms my fingers.
But something in my chest tightens—
a quiet constriction, like I've just been asked to breathe without lungs.

I look down into the dark surface of the tea.

And say, almost to the cup:

"That everything will fall apart.
That I'll disappoint everyone.
That…I'll disappear."

Ram Dass nods.

Not like a man who agrees—
but like one who *remembers*.

"That's the ego's bargain," he says gently.
'Let me stay in charge, and I'll keep you visible.
Lovable.
Needed.'

He pauses.

"But what it never tells you is the cost."

The fire pops once.
Sharp.
Sudden.
Like punctuation.

I whisper, "What is the cost?"

Adler doesn't answer right away.
He sets his tea down.
Folds his hands in his lap.

And then—
just one word at a time:

"Presence.
Peace.
Wholeness."

He looks at me.

"The very things you're working so hard to earn."

The words don't land in my mind.
They land in my gut.
Like truth I already knew—
but didn't want to name.

∞

I stare at the logs in the hearth,
watching them collapse into ash.

They don't resist.
They don't cling to form.
They simply give themselves to formlessness—
like it was always the plan.

There's something mesmerizing about it.
Not just beautiful.
True.

Ram Dass's voice breaks the silence,
but not the stillness.

"Control is the last illusion we let go of," he says.
"It's the ego's final trick.
Not out of arrogance, but out of fear.

It says: If I let go, I'll fall apart.
But the deeper truth is this:
It's the holding on that's breaking you.
Letting go isn't the weakness.
It's the beginning of trust.
The first breath of freedom.

We cling to it, thinking it keeps us safe.

But really…
it keeps us small."

The words float.
They don't demand anything.
But something inside me loosens anyway.

I exhale.
Not because I chose to.
But because I'd been holding my breath for years.

Adler speaks, not to add wisdom—
but like someone tracing the same truth with a
different finger.

"And yet," he says,
"courage doesn't mean never being afraid.
It means choosing something higher than fear.
It means allowing yourself to not know—
and still stepping forward."

I don't respond.
I can't.

Because everything in me is…
trembling.
Not shaking.
Just—trembling.

Like something is about to break,
but not in a destructive way.
In a returning way.

I glance at both men.
They're not watching me.
They're holding space for something I haven't
seen yet.

I look down at my hands.
They feel foreign.

*How many choices had I made out of fear?*
*How many identities had I stitched together—just to*
*feel in control?*

I don't ask the question to sound wise.

I ask it because it rises from the ache:

"What happens," I whisper,
"if I let it all go?"

Ram Dass doesn't answer like a teacher.
He smiles.
Not with conclusions.
With presence.

"You don't fall," he says.

A pause.

"You dissolve."

I don't understand what that means.

Not fully.

But something in me does.

Adler leans forward—slowly, elbows on his knees.
His voice is low, like it's reaching backward through
time.

"And what remains," he says,
"is who you were
before you learned
to be afraid."

The words don't land in my mind.

They land in the body
beneath the body.
The one that remembers.

Something warm begins to spread in my chest.
Not joy.
Not even relief.

Just peace.
A peace that doesn't explain itself.

Like a hand on my shoulder that says,
*It's time.*

And for the first time, I don't need to hold the reins.
I don't need to steer the mystery.

Because I'm not separate from it.

I am the mystery—
being lived.

∞

Ram Dass leans forward and nudges a log into place.
The embers flare.
Sparks rise like fireflies startled from sleep—
and for a moment, everything glows.

Then it settles again.
The quiet crackle.
The slow pulse of heat.
The hush between stories.

"I remember the first time I really surrendered," he
says softly.
"Not just intellectually.
Not as a concept.
But in my body.
My heart."

His voice has shifted.
Not performing.
Just remembering.

"It was in India.
I was sitting on the ground in front of Maharaji.
And he looked at me the way no one ever had—
like I didn't need to prove a thing."

He pauses.
Not for effect—
but like he's back there.

"He didn't give me a formula.
He didn't explain enlightenment.
He told me to serve people.

To love them.
To see God in everything."

He smiles, but it's not a smile of clarity.
It's the kind you give when you finally stop trying to understand.

"I thought he was giving me a spiritual riddle," he says.
"Turns out, he was giving me a way out."

Adler lets out a soft chuckle.
"The mind hates simplicity."

Ram Dass laughs too—gentle, knowing.
"Oh, it loathes it.
It wants layers and nuance and frameworks.
It wants interpretation over intimacy.
But the soul…"
He trails off.

Then quietly:

"The soul just wants to love.
And be loved."

They both look at me.

But they don't pressure.
They *wait*.

And that's when I feel it again.

That tightening.

Not in the room.
Inside me.

A familiar swell in my chest—
like something's rising to be released,
but my mind keeps wrestling it back down.

*Don't let go.*
*Don't lose control now.*
*You've come too far to fall apart.*

It's not them applying pressure.
It's me.
It's always been me.

The voice of the mind—
disguised as safety.
As intelligence.
As "holding it together."

But underneath that tightening…

There's something softer.

Something waiting.

Not to be explained—
to be felt.

∞

I set my tea down,
but my hand doesn't leave the cup.
It just rests there.

Like I'm holding on to the last small thing I can
control.

"I don't know how to let go," I say.
"I don't even know what it means."

My voice doesn't sound like mine.
It sounds younger.
Tighter.
Like it was pulled from the chest of a boy who
learned to survive by figuring everything out.

Adler doesn't jump in.
He lets the words hang like incense in the silence.

Then—gently:

"It means being willing to not know.
To stop managing the outcome.
To stop rehearsing who you are."

I want to ask what that looks like.
I want another cup of tea.
I want a framework.

But all I say is:

"But what if…
what's underneath the mask
isn't enough?"

Ram Dass leans in slightly.
His eyes don't blink.

"That's the ego's final thread," he says.
"The belief that if you stop performing…
you'll disappear."

He doesn't say it with force.
He says it like a man who's been there—
on the edge of that cliff.
And jumped.

The air thickens.

My chest tightens.
Not metaphorically.
Literally.
Like I'm bracing for the impact of my own
unraveling.

Adler speaks, slow and steady.

"Then you grieve," he says.
"You mourn the self you tried so hard to become.
The one who held it all together.
The one who kept everyone proud, or happy, or at a
distance."

He pauses.

"And in that mourning…
something real begins."

I don't speak.
I can't.

Because something *is* beginning.
Or maybe something is ending.
It's hard to tell the difference.

Ram Dass doesn't fill the silence.
He just lowers his voice to a whisper.

"This is the part," he says,
"where the ego dies a little."

He doesn't dress it up.
He doesn't call it transcendence.
He names it for what it is:

"It won't feel graceful.
It won't feel enlightened.
It'll feel like breaking."

And suddenly—
it does.

Not loudly.
Not all at once.
But from the inside.

A quiet collapse.
A letting go I didn't orchestrate.
Like a muscle that finally stopped clenching after
years of holding.

A breath I didn't mean to take.
A tremble I no longer try to hide.

No one rushes to name it.
They just stay.

And so do I.

∞

The tears come—
not in a wave,
not in a flood—
but like a soft rain after a long drought.

Not forced.
Not dramatic.
Just real.

Two or three.
Maybe more.
I don't count them.
For once, I'm not measuring anything.

No one moves to comfort me.
No one tells me it's okay.
They just stay.

Present.
Witnessing.

And for the first time in my life,
that's enough.

The room feels different now.
Not lighter.
Not heavier.
Just…truer.

The fire exhales a ribbon of smoke.
Outside, the wind presses gently against the
window—
not asking to come in,
just reminding us it's there.

Adler looks into the embers.
His voice is quiet,
like something offered to the flames more than
to me.

"People think surrender means weakness," he says.
"But it's the strongest thing you'll ever do.
Because it means you're willing to feel it all."

I nod—barely.

I don't have words.

I'm not inside a breakthrough.
I'm inside a stillness.
Like the hush between waves.
Like a truth that no longer needs explaining.

Ram Dass sits with me in the quiet.
He doesn't need to say anything.
But when he does,
his voice is tender.
Grounded.

"To feel it all," he says,
"is to finally come alive."

The sentence doesn't ignite anything in me.
It doesn't elevate.

It just *settles*.

Like earth over a seed.

I feel hollowed out.
But not empty.

More like something unnecessary
has been cleared away.

∞

Adler shifts in his seat.
Not abruptly—just a small, conscious settling.
Like even his body knows the tone has changed.

"There's a strength in softness," he says.
"But it takes time to trust it.
Especially for men raised to believe strength meant
silence.
Suppression.
Control."

His words don't carry shame.
Only understanding.

I nod.

Not because I agree—
but because the truth of it lives somewhere deep in
my bones.

Ram Dass grins, the kind of grin that holds stories.
"I used to think vulnerability was for people who
hadn't yet built their armor," he says.
"Then I realized—vulnerability is what lives
underneath the armor.
It's not the absence of protection.
It's the presence of courage."

Adler smirks. "That sounds like something a
therapist would cross-stitch into a pillow."

Ram Dass laughs. "Guilty. But I'd light incense next
to it, so it'd be okay."

And I laugh too.

But for the first time tonight,
it's not a laugh to deflect.
Not a performance.
Just…ease.

No mask.
No tension behind the eyes.
Just breath moving through a softening chest.

Something in me settles.
Not because I've figured anything out.
But because I've stopped trying to.

There's no revelation here.
No epiphany.
Just the quiet knowing that I don't have to be at war
with myself anymore.

And maybe that's all strength really is—
not power,
not posture,
but peace.

The kind that doesn't need to prove itself.
The kind that knows when to stay soft.
The kind that lets go of control
and lives in the letting go.

∞

Somewhere in the house,
a clock begins to chime.

Twelve slow, resonant strikes.

Not loud.
Not dramatic.
But steady.

Midnight.

The turning point.
The breath between death and rebirth.
The center of the night,
when the old has fallen away
and the new hasn't yet arrived.

No one says a word.

Ram Dass rises—slowly, reverently—
and stirs the fire one last time.
Ash shifts.

Sparks lift like soft stars,
then vanish into air.

Adler refills his cup without a word.
He moves without urgency.
Like the tea itself is part of the ritual.

I don't ask what comes next.

For once...I don't need to know.

The silence doesn't feel empty.
It feels full.
Pregnant with something unnamed.

I sip the tea.
Let it move through the body that's no longer
braced.
Let it warm what's been cracked open.

Outside, the wind moves through the trees.
Branches bow.
Not in fear.
In reverence.

I close my eyes.

And for the first time in my life—
I'm not preparing for what's ahead.
I'm not guarding what's behind.
I'm not strategizing how to hold it all together.

I'm just…

here.

And somehow—
that feels like a beginning.

# CHAPTER SIX
## *Ashes of the Old Name*

The room is quiet.

Not empty—
just emptied.
Like something old has been released,
and we're sitting inside what remains.

The fire has burned low.
Only a soft bed of coals glows beneath the ash—
no longer reaching upward,
just resting.

Outside, the stars are piercing.
Brighter now.
As if they've drawn a little closer,
listening.

Ram Dass leans forward slowly,
fingers gently adjusting a coal with the iron poker.
The motion is tender, almost ceremonial.

Adler pours another round of tea.
Not rushed.
Not routine.

Just a quiet offering.
A kind of hospitality for the soul.

No one speaks.

And the silence doesn't ache.
It blesses.

This is the space between identities.
Between names.
Between performances.

Not the death of a person—
but the death of the person I pretended to be.

Something in me feels lighter.
But not free.
Not yet.

It's the feeling right before the release.
The soft anticipation of grief that hasn't arrived.

I hold the cup in both hands,
and I notice—I'm not bracing anymore.

No one is asking anything of me.
Not even me.

For the first time tonight,
I realize:
the fire didn't die.
It just stopped performing.

∞

I don't know how to describe it exactly.
It's not sadness.
Not fear.
It's quieter than that.

Like a tide going out,
taking something with it that I never said
goodbye to.

I stare into the cup again.
The steam is gone now.
Just warmth, fading slowly.

"I've never had someone close to me die," I say
quietly.
"Not yet."

Ram Dass doesn't move.
He just listens.
As if my voice is part of the fire.

"But lately," I continue,
"I feel like I've been grieving someone anyway."

Adler's gaze softens.
"Who?"

I pause.

And then:
"Me.
The version of me I thought I had to be."

The words don't come from my mouth.
They come from somewhere deeper.
A remembering I didn't know I carried.

"I've spent so much time building him.
Polishing him.
Defending him."

I look down.

"I don't even know when I stopped being him.
But he's gone.
And I don't think I ever let myself mourn it."

Ram Dass nods slowly.
"Just because there's no funeral,
doesn't mean there's no death."

Adler adds,
"And sometimes that's the harder one.
Because no one brings flowers.
No one tells you it's okay to fall apart.
You just…stop being who you were.
And hope someone notices."

I swallow.
Hard.

"I notice," I whisper.
"I miss him.
And I don't."

There's a long pause.
Long enough to feel like prayer.

And then I speak again, softer this time.
"I carried him for so long.
Gave him my name.
My voice.
My skin."

I exhale.

"I built my life around making him acceptable.
Lovable.
Unbreakable."

My hands tighten slightly around the cup.

"But I never asked if he was real.
Or just…necessary."

Ram Dass's voice comes like a hand on my back.
"You're not becoming someone new," he says.
"You're remembering someone ancient."

The fire shifts slightly—
as if it heard him.

And something in me whispers—not a thought, but
a knowing:
*This is your funeral, too.*

Maybe not for your body.
But for the one you pretended to be.

The one who smiled to be accepted.
Who performed to be safe.
Who hustled to be loved.

If you've never mourned them,
maybe you still carry them.

And maybe…
you don't need to anymore.

∞

Adler leans back, his gaze steady.
"Most people don't cling to certainty because they're
arrogant," he says.
"They cling to it because they're afraid."

I nod slowly.
Not because I'm thinking.
But because I remember.

"I was raised to be certain," I say.
"Certain we were right, and others were wrong.
Certain about what came after death.
Certain who was in, who was out.
Heaven. Hell.
The map was handed to me early."

Ram Dass watches me, gentle and unmoved.
"And did the map bring you peace?" he asks softly.

I pause.
"No," I say.
"It brought order.
It brought approval.
It brought clarity."

A breath.

"But it didn't bring peace."

Outside, the wind brushes against the window.
The fire pulses low and steady.
Everything in the room seems to be listening.

"I remember being a kid," I say,
"thinking I was supposed to believe the right things
about God, about sin, about eternity…
or people would go to hell.
Including me."

Adler tilts his head, not unkindly.
"A heavy crown for a child."

Ram Dass smiles gently.
"Ah…the American spiritual inheritance."

I chuckle, but there's no laughter in it.
"It gave me language.
It gave me a frame.
And I'm grateful for that.
But…"

The words trail off.

Adler finishes for me:
"But it didn't give you permission to wonder."

I nod.
"And it didn't give me permission to feel."

The fire cracks quietly—like punctuation.

Ram Dass's voice returns like warm wind.
"We don't just cling to belief systems.
We wear them like life vests.
Because underneath all that certainty…"

He pauses.

"…is chaos.
And most of us were never taught how to swim."

∞

The fire has dimmed again.
Not out—just low.
As if it's conserving its heat for what comes next.

I lean back in my chair,
feeling the steam from the tea on my lips
but not drinking it yet.

"There was a time," I say slowly,
"when I thought I had it all figured out.
God. Life. Salvation.
It was all so…clean."

Ram Dass doesn't flinch.
He doesn't smile either.
Just listens.
Fully.

"I remember defending my beliefs like they were my blood.
Quoting verses.

Correcting people.
Praying for their souls."

I look down.

"I thought I was saving them.
But really…
I was just trying to save myself from the fear of
being wrong."

Adler says nothing.
Not because he has nothing to add—
but because the silence says more.

Ram Dass eventually speaks.
"Letting go of certainty," he says,
"is a kind of death."

I nod.
Tears threaten—but don't fall.
Not yet.

"It was easier when I had a story," I whisper.
"Even if it didn't fit.
Even if it hurt."

Adler leans forward, his elbows on his knees.
"There's no ceremony for that loss," he says.
"No goodbye party when the scaffolding crumbles."

I breathe in sharply.
Not from pain.
From recognition.

"There should be," I say.

Ram Dass's eyes shine a little brighter.
"There should be," he echoes.
"Because it's not just a belief you lost.
It was a whole identity.
A belonging.
A worldview."

He pauses.
"And sometimes, the loneliness that follows isn't because God left…
but because we don't know how to reach for God without the scaffolding."

Adler speaks again, low and warm.
"When something sacred breaks,
the pieces still carry the sacred.
But now it's scattered.
And it takes time to gather it again."

I close my eyes.
And for the first time,
I let myself grieve
not just what I lost—
but how alone I've felt
since losing it.

∞

The room is quiet again.
Not solemn.
Just…aware.
Like even the fire knows where we're about to go.

I stare into it.
Watch a small ember collapse into ash.
And something in me collapses, too.

"I don't think I wanted to die," I say softly.
"Not really."
My voice doesn't shake.
It's too tired for that.

"I just didn't want to keep *being* like this."

Ram Dass doesn't ask what I mean.
He already knows.

"There was a time," I continue,
"when I was in Costa Rica.
From the outside, it looked like a retreat.
A reset.
I told people I needed clarity, space, stillness."

I pause.

"But I wasn't seeking clarity.
I was collapsing."

I exhale slowly, eyes on the fire.
"There was this one night.
I was lying in a hammock, staring out into the
jungle.
The moon was high.
I could hear the strings of a guitar in the
background, but I couldn't feel anything.
Not awe.

Not peace.
Not fear.
Just…nothing."

Adler watches me.
Doesn't speak.

"I remember thinking,
*Maybe I don't need to go home.*
Not in some dramatic way.
Just…
maybe I could dissolve right here."

Ram Dass doesn't flinch.
He just nods, reverently.

"I don't think I was suicidal," I continue.
"I just didn't want to keep living as the life I had built.
The version of me who always had the answers.
Who held it all together.
I was so tired of holding it."

The words fall like stones into still water.

No one tries to rescue me.
No one hands me a brighter thought.
They just sit.

And in that silence,
I feel something rise to the surface.
A truth I hadn't dared name.

"I wasn't trying to end my life.
I was trying to end the performance."

Ram Dass's eyes soften.
"And did you?"

I nod, barely.
"It felt as though everything but my breath had ended."

Adler's voice is low, but sure.
"And that ending…
wasn't destruction.
It was permission."

Ram Dass leans in, elbows on his knees.
"You didn't want to die," he says.
"You wanted the mask to fall.
You wanted to feel something real.
That's not darkness.
That's longing."

He pauses, then adds:
"And longing is one of the most sacred forces in the universe."

∞

The fire has quieted again—
a soft bed of coals, low and alive.

The room breathes with something ancient.
Not heavy.
Just still.

"There was a time," I say,
"when I thought I'd tried everything."

Ram Dass tilts his head, gently curious.

"Therapy. Religion. Breathwork. Meditation.
Books. Retreats. Coaches. Plant medicine."

I pause.
"My first ayahuasca ceremony was in Costa Rica.
It shook something loose in me—
something I didn't even know was trapped."

Adler doesn't blink.
He just nods, slowly.
Like someone who's seen people name their ghosts
before.

"For the first time," I continue,
"everything I thought I was...collapsed.
The stories.
The striving.
The scaffolding."

I remember sitting at the feet of the shaman,
Looking up at them after hours of sitting with the
medicine,
feeling sick to my stomach.

I reached for words.
I always had words.
I had none. I suddenly had no idea who I was.
I was physically becoming ill in that moment.

It's as if I was suddenly back in Costa Rica, sitting in
the maloca at the feet of the shaman,
reaching for words,
and instead,
finding truth.

Ram Dass's eyes shine.
"I remember that collapse," he says.
"For me, it was psilocybin. LSD.
The first time I let go, I thought I had died.
And all I felt…was relief.
Like, *thank God, I don't have to be 'me' anymore.*"

He laughs gently.

"But here's what I learned," he continues.
"Psychedelics are not the answer.
They are the invitation."

He leans forward.
"Maharaji walked me through the door.
But I needed that rupture to remember there *was* a
door."

I nod, slowly.
"That's what ayahuasca did for me.
It was a crack.
A rupture of some kind."

Ram Dass smiles.
"And the real work began after, didn't it?"

I smile back.
"Yeah.

The integration.
The ordinary moments.
Learning to stop escaping into experience—
and start embodying the truth it showed me."

Adler folds his hands.
"Every method has its season," he says.
"But if we're not careful, we mistake the method for the miracle."

Ram Dass chuckles.
"Alan Watts said it best:
*Don't mistake the finger pointing at the moon for the moon.*"

His voice softens.
"We cling to the finger.
The book.
The teacher.
The religion.
The identity.
Because it feels solid."

He pauses.
"But we weren't meant to worship the pointing.
We were meant to look."

Silence.
Then Adler, gently:
"And what happens when you finally look?"

I exhale.

"I don't see a thing.
I feel something."

"What do you feel?" Ram Dass asks.

I place my hand on my chest.

"Home."

∞

No one speaks for a while.
The fire murmurs low,
casting long shadows along the stone wall.

The tea still warm,
But none of us reach for it.

It feels like we've crossed into some quiet place
inside the night—
a place where even breath feels ceremonial.

Ram Dass finally breaks the silence,
but his voice is softer now.
Like he's speaking to something not just in me,
but in all of us.

"There's a kind of death," he says,
"that isn't the end of life—
but the end of illusion."

His eyes are fixed on the coals, glowing faintly in the
hearth.
"When the roles we've played
get too tight…

when the stories can't hold us anymore…
the ego begins to fray."

Adler nods.
"I've seen it too.
People come to therapy thinking they're broken.
But often, what's breaking isn't them.
It's the false goal they were never meant to carry."

He leans forward.

"The marriage they modeled from their parents.
The faith that was never truly theirs.
The man or woman they thought they had to
become
to earn love."

I inhale slowly, something catching in my chest.

"And when that false self begins to die…"
I pause, feeling it more than saying it.
"…there's no funeral."

Ram Dass turns toward me.

"But there should be," he says.
"Because grief isn't just for what we lose.
It's for what we wore to survive."

I close my eyes.

"I used to think something was wrong with me," I
whisper.

"For feeling like I wanted to disappear.
For craving an ending I couldn't explain."

Adler doesn't interrupt.

"And now I wonder," I continue,
"…maybe I didn't want to die.
Maybe I just wanted to stop pretending."

Ram Dass leans in again, elbows resting on his knees.
"That's not despair," he says.
"That's the soul asking for truth."

He lets the words linger, then adds—

"You didn't want to be gone.
You wanted to *return*.
To yourself.
To love.
To God."

Adler exhales slowly.
"Ego death feels like dying.
Because it is.
But what survives…
is what was true all along."

I sit in the stillness,
and let those words break something open in me.

Not loudly.
Not completely.

Just enough
to feel like a door has opened
where a wall once was.

∞

The fire shifts—barely.
A soft exhale of heat.
Like even it is beginning to rest.

Ram Dass leans back in his chair.
There's a quiet ease in his face now.
Not a conclusion.
Just presence.

"The game isn't to be right," he says.
"Or happy. Or euphoric."

He pauses.

"The game is to be free."

Adler folds his hands in his lap.
"And to be free," he adds,
"you have to stop numbing your feelings.
And stop being ruled by them too."

I nod, barely.
There's no performance left in me.
No need to understand it all right now.

"There's a cost to staying numb," I whisper.
"It feels safer. But it also makes everything…flat."

Ram Dass watches me with eyes that don't flinch.

"You can't heal what you won't feel," he says gently.
"And you can't feel when you're still performing."

I inhale through my nose.
Exhale slowly.
And finally say the thing I hadn't yet admitted:

"I've spent most of my life intellectualizing my pain.
Naming it.
Framing it.
Making sense of it."

Adler smiles, not unkindly.
"That's a survival strategy.
And a brilliant one."

Ram Dass leans forward.

"But freedom lives in the body," he says.
"In the ache you stop resisting.
In the tears you don't apologize for.
In the joy that doesn't need a reason."

My chest tightens.

I want to cry.
But not from sadness.

From relief.

Adler speaks into the quiet.

"We don't start healing when we finally understand
our pain.

We start healing when we stop needing to explain it."

A long silence follows.
No one rushes to fill it.

And in that space,
something shifts in me.

The ache I've carried for years
no longer feels like the enemy.

It feels like a guide.

And for the first time in a long time,
I don't feel like I need to *get over* anything.

I just need to stay.
Breathe.
Feel.

That's enough.

# CHAPTER SEVEN
## *The Space Between Names*

The fire has quieted again—
There is a stillness that follows surrender.
Not the calm of victory—
but the hush after something has fallen apart.

The fire is low now.
No crackle. No flash.
Just a quiet orange breath in the dark.

Outside, the sky holds itself in silence.
The stars aren't rushing to say anything.

Neither are we.

Ram Dass sits with his palms open on his lap.
Adler hasn't spoken in several minutes.
And I—

I don't know who I am anymore.
And for the first time, I'm not trying to answer that.

I don't feel brave.
I don't feel wise.
I don't feel anything I can name.

But I feel…here.

And somehow, that feels like enough.

For so long, I thought awakening would feel like
arrival.
Like clarity.
Like becoming someone new.

But it feels more like this:

Like losing all the names you were taught to answer
to,
and not rushing to replace them.

Like staring into a fire
and not needing to say what it means.

Like sitting in a room with people who expect
nothing from you—
and realizing you don't have to perform to belong.

There's a softness to this kind of silence.
It doesn't demand.
It just waits.

And maybe this is the holy pause
we've been taught to avoid.

The space between identities.
The breath between lives.
The moment between "was" and "becoming."

The place where the soul doesn't need a label—
because it's finally being heard.

Not for what it can explain.

But for what it is.

∞

The silence stretches long enough
that I almost forget we're still sitting together.

But no one is uncomfortable.

There's no performance in the room now.
No roles.
No right thing to say.

And maybe that's why it feels so sacred.

I glance down at my hands.
They're resting in my lap.
Not clenched.
Not performing.

Just…resting.

Ram Dass stirs slightly.
Not to speak.
Just to breathe.

Adler remains still, like he's listening to something
deeper than sound.

And then—softly, without warning—I say it:

"I don't know who I am."

My voice doesn't shake.
It's not a crisis.
It's a confession.

Adler doesn't nod.
Doesn't comfort.

He just receives it.

Ram Dass smiles, slow and knowing.

"Good," he whispers.

Then nothing.

Just the fire breathing its low, rhythmic breath.

I lean forward slightly.
Not in urgency.
But in honesty.

"I used to be so many things," I say.
"A leader. A teacher. A fixer. A Christian. A seeker.
A coach. A manly man. An athlete. A strong one. A
broken one. A man trying to be good. A man trying
to be free."

The words come slowly now, like stones I'm setting
down one at a time.

"I needed those names.
They helped me feel real.
They helped me feel safe."

Adler's voice is barely above a breath.

"And now?"

I exhale.
Long.
Quiet.

"And now...
they feel too small."

Ram Dass leans toward the fire and lifts a log into place.

The flames rise—steady, unhurried.
Not eager.
Just alive.

Then, a sudden crack—sharp and bright—
Demanding the attention of the room.

"You're not those names," he says, watching the light.
"And you never were."

He turns to me.

"Not this," he says.

Then nods toward the silence.

"Not that."

His smile softens. "Neti, neti."

I close my eyes.
The words land somewhere deeper than my mind.
Somewhere older.

Not this.
Not that.

Just…this.

Breath.
Awareness.
A presence that doesn't need a title to be true.

And maybe this is what the soul has been waiting
for all along:

To not be understood—
but felt.

To not be labeled—
but known.

To not be useful—
but free.

∞

Ram Dass smiles again, watching my face.
Not like he's trying to teach—
but like he knows what's rising in me.

"Neti, neti," he says again.

"Not this.
Not that."

He lets the words linger like smoke.

Then, gently:
"It's an old practice. From the Upanishads.
A way of remembering who we are
by letting go of everything we're not."

I nod, slowly.

But something in me still wants to *know*.
To land on something.
To belong to something.

Adler senses it.
His voice is low, steady. "We don't just cling to
identities because we like them.
We cling to them because they were *given* to us—
before we even had a choice."

Ram Dass leans back, his voice like warm honey.

"Some names were whispered into you before you
could speak.
Good boy.
Strong one.
Sinner.
Chosen.
Saved.
Broken.
Promising."

He pauses.

"None of them were yours.
Not really.
They were maps handed to you
by well-meaning people who were *figuring it out*
themselves."

I swallow, eyes locked on the fire.

"I've carried those names my whole life.
Worn them like skin.
Some of them felt true.
Some felt like lies I had to live up to.
But they all felt *heavy*."

Ram Dass nods, slowly.

"They weren't meant to be carried.
Only passed through.
Like doorways."

"Even sacred names—'child of God,' 'lightworker,'
'leader'—can become armor when they replace the
quiet knowing beneath them. What begins as truth
becomes performance the moment we forget we
were already whole."

Adler adds, "And when we confuse the doorway for
the destination, we get stuck."

I look into the flames.

"I'm tired of being stuck."

No one rushes to fix it.

Instead, Ram Dass says softly,
"Then let the names fall.
Even the good ones.
Even the sacred ones."

Adler's voice follows like a gentle tide.
"You're not here to build a better mask.
You're here to find the face beneath all of them."

Silence wraps the room again.
Not cold—
but *true*.

I feel the stirrings of something ancient.
A loosening.
A remembering.

And in that silence, I wonder—
not what I will become…

…but who I was
before they told me who to be.

∞

I don't speak for a while.

No one does.

It feels like the fire is speaking now—
murmuring in low crackles, rising in bursts, then
settling back down.
There's something almost mischievous in it.
Like it's telling a joke only the room can hear.

I smirk without meaning to,
picturing the flames dancing just to see if anyone's
watching.

I'm not sure how much time passes.
The clock isn't part of this room anymore.

I sit with my palms resting open.
Not meditating.
Not doing anything.

Just being…
without a name to answer to.

And it's disorienting.
Like floating in deep water and not knowing which
way is up.

And suddenly, I'm not in this room.
I'm back in a conference room—
fluorescent lights, glass walls like in a fish bowl, a
tray of semi-toasted bagels and lukewarm coffee.

We're doing a team-building exercise, flipping
through our StrengthsFinder results.
Each of us clutching the printout like it holds some
secret code to who we are.

The facilitator reads one profile at a time aloud.
We pretend to act casual, but everyone is waiting—
waiting for their turn to be named.
To be revealed.
To be understood.

When she finally gets to mine, I sit up straighter.
I nod along, trying to stay humble—
but inside, I'm buzzing.
Hungry for the words that might finally explain me
to the room.
Hungry to be seen.
And maybe more than anything…to be validated.

To hear someone say, "Yes. That's you."
And believe it.
Even if I'm not sure I do.
Even if the part they're describing is just the mask
I've mastered.

I blink.
The fire hasn't moved.
But I have.

Adler finally speaks.

"This is the part most people rush past."

His voice is calm. Familiar now.
Like a hand on the back of the neck.

"The ego doesn't mind letting go of old names—
so long as it can trade them for new ones."

Ram Dass chuckles gently.
"It'll even trade for spiritual names.
'Awakened.
Enlightened.
Healer.

Seeker.
Embodied.'"

He turns toward me. His eyes are soft, steady.

"But the soul doesn't want a better name.
It wants freedom."

I nod, slowly.
But my chest is tight again.
I didn't expect that.

Adler sees it.

"What's happening in your body?" he asks.

I close my eyes.

"My stomach's tense.
My chest feels…like I'm falling.
Like if I let go completely, I'll disappear."

Ram Dass smiles with something close to reverence.

"That's the illusion."

He leans in slightly.

"You're not disappearing.
You're just no longer being *contained*."

Adler adds, "The falling feeling—it's grief and awe at
once.
You're not losing yourself.
You're meeting yourself.

The part that was never separate from God to begin with."

I breathe slowly.
Something opens.

Not an answer.

A *space*.

I don't know who I am.
But I'm not afraid of the not-knowing anymore.

It's holy here.
Wide.
Strange.
Still.

And maybe this is the new beginning—
not with a name,
but with a silence
that no longer needs to be filled.

∞

The room is so quiet now,
I can hear the tea settling in my cup.

No lessons.
No breakthroughs.
Just the warmth of presence.

And in that quiet, I remember something.
Not a big moment.
Not some mystical vision or awakening.

Just…

A memory.

I was thirty-three, sitting in the passenger seat of my
friend's old F-150.
We'd just left a concert.
My head was full. My chest, hollow.
I was in one of those seasons where everything
looked generally okay on the outside
and nothing made sense on the inside.

I don't remember what I said.
But I remember how he looked at me.

He didn't try to fix it.
He didn't offer advice.
He didn't turn up the music.

He just looked at me—really looked—
like he saw the whole war behind my eyes
and didn't need me to explain it.

And something in me cracked.

Not in a dramatic way.
No tears. No declarations.

But I felt it.

That someone could witness my pain without
needing to repair it.

That I could be *seen* without needing to be understood.

That maybe God wasn't waiting in a church—
but was sitting beside me in an F-150.
with a friend who didn't need to say a word.

I wasn't calling it God at that time.

But looking back now?

It was the first time I felt truly held
by something bigger than me.

Something that didn't need a name.

Something that didn't flinch when I didn't know mine.

"Most of us don't know when we're being held.
Not until much later,
when the memory glows in our chest
and says: *That was Love, too.*"

Ram Dass lifts his cup to his lips, as if he's heard the memory without me saying it.

He smiles gently. "That's how it happens."

Adler's voice follows like a quiet echo.
"Perhaps, God shows up most clearly
when we stop looking in the ways we were
taught to."

The fire flickers.
The night thickens.

And I realize—
I haven't lost God.

I've just outgrown the story that said where God
lived.

∞

I was taught God had an address.
A building.
A book.
A system of right beliefs.

I was taught He had rules.
Preferences.
A fragile ego.
A ledger.

I was taught He was a He.

And if I followed the right path,
prayed the right way,
believed the right things,
denied the wrong ones…

I'd be loved.
Saved.
Safe.

But I wasn't safe.
Not in the ways that mattered.

Because somewhere along the way,
God became a performance.

And I became an actor in my own spiritual life.

I learned how to lift my hands in worship
without knowing how to ask for help.

I knew how to pray publicly
but not how to speak the truth in my own bedroom.

I could say *God is love*
and still believe I was unlovable.

Ram Dass watches me quietly.

"You were given a frame," he says gently,
"before you were allowed to meet the mystery."

Adler adds, "And then you had to decide—stay
inside the frame...
or meet God somewhere wilder."

I nod, slowly. "I didn't mean to leave the frame."

"I know," Ram Dass says. "You outgrew it."

Silence again.

"But here's what's strange," I say.
"I miss parts of it.
The beauty.
The devotion.
Even the songs."

Adler smiles gently. "It wasn't all false.
It just wasn't whole."

Ram Dass leans toward me, the firelight soft in his
eyes.
"The God you miss…was never the one who needed
the frame.
They were the one who sat with you in the back row
when you felt like a fraud.
The one who whispered to you through your doubt.
The one who waited quietly in your grief
long after the sermon ended."

He pauses.

"That God?
That God never left."

And I feel it—
not belief.
Not a return to something old.

But a presence.

A quiet assurance
that the sacred never needed my certainty.

Only my openness.

The sacred doesn't need me to understand.
It just needs me to stay.

∞

I used to think God was found in the holding together.
In the discipline.
In the devotion.
In the strength to keep showing up.

But lately?

God keeps showing up in the *coming undone.*

In the tremble.
In the doubt.
In the tears I didn't schedule.
In the prayers I never said out loud.

I feel it most in the moments that don't fit the story.
The breakdowns.
The silence.
The grief I can't explain.

That's where the sacred keeps cracking through.

Adler lifts his cup, his eyes steady.

"There's a holiness to rupture," he says.
"When the scaffolding collapses—
it can feel like failure.
But it's often the beginning of *truth.*"

Ram Dass nods.

"Most people think awakening is about building something brighter.
But it's not.

It's about letting what was never real fall apart—
so the light can *get in.*"

I look into the fire.
"I feel like I've broken a hundred times already."

The words fall out without force.
Not a cry for help—
just a quiet truth surfacing.

For a moment, the room feels even stiller.
And inside me, something stirs.

A question I haven't dared ask:
*Is there anything left to shape?*

I don't speak it aloud.
But I feel its echo in my chest.

Ram Dass leans in, smiling softly.
"Good," he says. "That means you're soft enough to
be shaped.
Only clay that's been broken can be reshaped on the
wheel."

Adler adds, "And only hearts that have been cracked
can hold others without judgment."

I breathe slowly.
Something inside me loosens again.

I'm not being punished.
I'm being opened.

Not by force.
But by love I wasn't ready for
until everything else had failed.

∞

The fire has burned low again.
No flames now—just embers.
Breathing.
Glowing.
Alive, even in stillness.

I feel different.

Not new.
Not fixed.
But *here*.

The ache hasn't left.
But it no longer feels like a problem to solve.
It feels like a doorway.

Ram Dass lifts his eyes to the window.

"The mind wants closure," he says.
"It wants to land somewhere.
But the soul…
the soul just wants to *wonder*."

Adler smiles. "We're not meant to master the mystery.
We're meant to *make space* for it."

I sip my tea again.
It tastes the same.
And somehow, completely different.

I think of all the names I've carried.
All the masks I wore to earn love.
All the roles I confused with who I am.

And I feel something rise—
not pride.
Not even peace.

Just awe.

That I'm still here.

That I can let go, and still be held.

That God didn't need me to understand Him
before letting me feel Him.

Outside, the wind moves gently through the trees.

Inside, the fire hums.

Ram Dass leans forward.

"Wonder is what's left," he says,
"when control dies and love survives."

Adler adds, "And wonder is how the soul remembers
itself."

I close my eyes.

And for the first time in a long time...
I don't need a plan.
I don't need a title.
I don't need a name.

I just want to be here.
With the mystery.
With the fire.
With whatever this is—this presence that keeps
loving me
even when I forget how to love myself.

Enough.

And I think—maybe for the first time—
that might be enough.

# CHAPTER EIGHT
## *What Now Wants to Live*

The fire hasn't gone out.
But something in the room has changed.
Less a place of burning—
more a place of warmth.
The kind you gather around, not to be changed,
but simply to be.

Outside, the night is beginning to soften.
There's no sunrise yet—
but something is shifting.
The stars don't feel quite so far away.

No one says much.
The room isn't thick with grief anymore.
It's not heavy.
It's tender.

Ram Dass leans back into his chair like a man who
trusts the floor beneath him.
Adler's hands rest open now, not folded.

And me?

I feel like I've just emerged from deep water.
Not gasping—

but blinking.
Breathing again.
Tasting air like it's new.

There's still ache.
Still the ache.
But it's quieter.
And underneath it, something else.
Something I haven't felt in a long time.
Not peace. Not joy.
Not even purpose.

Just…curiosity.
A flicker.
A whisper.

*What now wants to live?*

Adler notices it. He always does.
"You feel different," he says, not as a question.
I nod, slowly. "I do."
"What's present?"
I sit with the question.
Then smile, just barely. "I don't know…but I'm
listening."
Ram Dass grins, his voice soft and warm.
"That's the beginning of every good story."

The fire breathes. So do I.
And I feel it:
Not a calling, exactly.
More like a remembering.

Like something just under the surface,
waiting for me to be soft enough to hear it.

For the first time in a long time,
I don't need to define myself.
I don't need to rebuild a new identity
to replace the old one that fell apart.
I just want to follow the thread.

Not to impress.
Not to perform.
But to see where it leads.

What wants to move through me now?
What wants to be touched, tasted, spoken?

What wants to be created?

I stay quiet, listening.
And then—

Something shifts inside me.
Not a revelation.
Not a breakthrough.
Just a flicker.

Like the breath before a word.
The spark before a flame.
The way your fingers twitch in your sleep before you
fully wake.

It's subtle. Easy to miss.
But it's there.

Not ambition.
Not striving.
Not a goal to reach.

Just…curiosity.

I lean forward, hands around my tea.
"I feel like something's coming alive again," I say.
"But I don't know what it is."

Ram Dass smiles, eyes soft. "It doesn't have to be
named."
Adler adds, "Or rushed."

There's a quiet between them.
A space that honors the smallness of this moment.

"Let it be blurry," Ram Dass says.
"Let it be delicate," Adler echoes.

I nod slowly.
"I don't feel driven. Not like before.
But I do feel drawn.
Like a thread tugging soft at my ribs.
And I want to follow it."

Ram Dass sets his cup down, gentle as always.
"That's how it begins," he says.
"Not with a thunderclap.
But with a whisper."

He glances at the fire.
"The ego builds with comparison.
The soul creates with wonder."

Adler leans back slightly, as if giving my words space to settle.

"You don't need to know what's next," he says. "Just stay in relationship with what's alive."

Alive.

The word lands.

Not urgent.
Not performative.
Just true.

And I realize—
I'm not rebuilding.
I'm listening.

Listening to the part of me that was never destroyed.
Only buried.
Only quieted.
Only waiting.

Not for the right moment.
But for the right presence.

And now, with my hands warm from the cup,
and my body tired but soft,
I feel it again:
The ache to create.
Not to impress.
Not to prove.
But to become.

To become what I already am.

If I would only let it rise.

There's something tender about this ache.

Not the ache of longing for what was lost—
but the ache of something stirring,
of something waiting to be born.

It doesn't feel urgent.
It doesn't feel loud.
But it's steady.

A thrum beneath the ribs.
A quiet pulse in the palms.
A whisper on the edges of breath.

Ram Dass watches me—not with expectation,
but with that unbearable kindness again.
The kind that sees not what you should be doing—
but who you already are.

"There's a reason it feels like an ache," he says gently.
"It's not because you're lacking.
It's because you're full."
He pauses. "Full of something that's ready to move
through you."

Adler lifts his eyes. "Creation isn't always a firework.
Sometimes it's just the first inhale
after a long time holding your breath."

I feel that.
Somewhere deep.

"I thought I had to figure out what to do with my life," I whisper.
"But maybe I just need to ask what life wants to do with me."

The room stills again.

And I feel it:
This ache isn't a problem.
It's a companion.
It's the soul's way of asking,
Will you let me speak now?

Ram Dass closes his eyes for a moment,
as if listening to something inside him.
"When I first started teaching," he says,
"I thought it was my job to have something to say.
But the longer I've listened,
the more I've realized—my only job is to be a space
where something true can arrive."

Adler nods. "That's the shift.
From being a performer of your life
to being a participant in it."

The ache grows warmer now.
Not pain. Not pressure.
More like warmth against the skin.
Like a hand on your back, saying: Go on.
I'm with you.

And I realize—
this is the beginning of creation.

Not in output,
but in permission.
A transmission.
As if tuning to a sugnal.

To let the ache be holy.
To let it guide me.
To let it shape me from the inside out.

Not toward a role.
Not toward a plan.

But toward something felt and alive.

Something only I can bring.
Because it was never mine to hoard.
Only mine to carry.

And maybe…to offer.

Outside, the wind moves through the trees like
breath through lungs.

The night is still here—
but it's different now.

Less a shadow,
more a cloak.

The kind you wrap around your shoulders
when you're about to step out into something new.

Ram Dass hasn't said much for a while.
Neither has Adler.

It doesn't feel like withholding.
It feels like respect.

Like they know what's happening inside me
isn't theirs to guide anymore.

It's mine to answer.

And something is answering—
not in words,
but in a feeling I don't know how to name.
It's not a decision. It's a readiness.

Something wants to live.

I don't mean survive.
I don't mean exist.

I mean *live*.

Like a color wants to be painted.
Like a song wants to be sung.
Like an ocean wants to crash against the shore
just because it can.

Adler finally speaks, his voice low and true.
"There's a turning point we all reach," he says.
"When the desire to stay hidden is still there—
but something deeper wants to be seen more."

Ram Dass adds, "It's not that the fear disappears.
It's that your soul stops asking for permission."

When the pull toward your truth
becomes stronger than the guilt of abandoning your
disguise.

I exhale.

It's not time to act yet.
Not quite.

But the readiness is there.
In the way I sit.
In the way I breathe.
In the way my fingers curl slightly at the thought of
holding a pen again.

Or opening my mouth.
Or stepping outside barefoot in the dark,
just to feel the earth and say: I'm still here.

The fire hums.
The coals pulse.
And I feel it in my chest again—
not clarity,
not certainty,

but *yes.*

A holy yes.
A quiet yes.
A yes that doesn't need proof,
because it knows its own root.

And maybe that's all creation ever asked for—
not mastery.
Not perfection.

Just *willingness.*

A soul soft enough to listen.
A heart brave enough to stay open.
A body willing to carry wonder forward.

Even into the unknown.

Especially into the unknown.

This is not the self I tried to become.
This is the self that remained after everything else
was surrendered.
And he's ready to create.

# CHAPTER NINE

## *The Invitation to Create*

✦

The night is thinning.

The sky hasn't shifted color yet—
but the air is different.
The kind of different you feel in your skin
before your eyes can name it.

There's a quiet expectancy in the room.
Like something is gathering just beneath the surface.
Like the ground itself is leaning in.

Ram Dass hasn't spoken in a while.
But his silence feels alive.
Like a well that has learned not to speak too soon.
Adler sits nearby, his eyes soft, distant—
like he's watching a horizon only he can see.

And me?

Something in me is humming.
Not loudly. Not urgently.
But like the low drone of a cello string—
tuned, waiting.

It's not the hum of anxiety.
It's the hum of potential.

Of readiness.

I close my eyes.
And I hear it—not a voice,
but a question blooming in my chest:

*What will I do with what I now know?*
Not as obligation.
But as offering.

For the first time in a long time,
I'm not asking what I should build.
I'm asking what wants to be born.

Not what I must prove.
But what I must give.

Ram Dass stirs, then speaks—quietly, clearly.

"You know, when I stopped trying to be somebody,
the most surprising thing happened.
I didn't become nobody.
I became a servant."

He looks at me. Not with intensity. With devotion.

"We don't create to become special.
We create because it's how love moves through us.
Service is not sacrifice. It's worship.
When it's real, it's not about helping others.
It's about dissolving the illusion that we're separate."

The words don't land like a task.
They land like truth.
The kind that loosens your shoulders
and calls your hands forward.

Adler lets the silence stretch,
then says, "We all long to matter.
And in the deepest sense, we do.
But meaning doesn't come from impact.
It comes from alignment."

He folds his hands in his lap.

"Create, not to be seen—
but because what is in you is too sacred to withhold."

The fire hums beside us.
And something begins to move in me.
Not the pressure to produce.
But the permission to respond.

To the ache.
To the gift.
To the thread I'm still following.

This isn't a performance anymore.

It's a prayer.

∞

Adler pours more tea, slow and unhurried.
Ram Dass doesn't speak. He's watching the steam
rise.

And something about the way they're both so still makes me realize—

They're not waiting for me to become anything.

They're just here.

With me.

With this.

With whatever wants to unfold.

I sit back, exhale, and place my hands flat against my thighs.
I can feel the heat in my palms. The pulse in my fingertips.
Not from anxiety—
from readiness.

"What if I don't know what I'm here to do?" I ask, not out of fear—
but truth.

Adler's eyes meet mine. "You're not here to do something impressive.
You're here to do something *true*."

Ram Dass adds, "And you'll know it's true because it won't feel like ambition.
It'll feel like *home*."

That lands.

Not in my mind. In my chest.

Because I've chased impressive.
I've played that game.
And every time I won, I felt further from myself.

But this?

This feels like a different kind of creation.
Not a brand. Not a performance.
A *life*. A soul-shaped expression of love.

I stare into the fire again.

"What if the only thing I'm here to do," I whisper,
"is let what's inside me…*live outside me?*"

Ram Dass smiles—soft and sure.
"Then do that," he says. "And let it be enough."
Adler nods. "That *is* contribution. That's meaning."

A long
…silence follows.

Not empty—
but full.
Like the room itself is bowing to something
unspoken.

And in that quiet, I realize:

I don't need a five-year plan.
I don't need a polished message or a ten-step
strategy.
I need to listen.

To keep listening.

To let the shape of my life form like clay in wet hands—
not from pressure,
but from presence.

To create as an act of worship.
To build as a form of devotion.
To let my days become my offering.

Not because I *have* to.
But because I *get* to.
Because I was made for this.
Because something holy is asking to be made visible—
and I'm finally ready to say yes.


∞

The night is quiet again.

But this time, the silence doesn't feel like stillness.

It feels like readiness.

Like the world is holding its breath—waiting.

Waiting not for something grand…

But something true.

Ram Dass shifts slightly in his seat, and it feels like a gesture of reverence, not restlessness. As if he knows we're close to something sacred now.

"You know," he says gently, "for most of my life, I thought my work was the offering."

He glances toward the fire.

"The talks. The books. The service. The legacy."

Then he turns back to me, eyes kind and steady.

"But that was never the offering. *I* was."

A pause.

"I had to learn that the most sacred thing I could ever offer…was my own transformation. My own aliveness. The truth of my being. That's what changes people. Not what you make—*who you become while making it.*"

Adler nods, slow and sure.

"It's tempting to think of contribution as outcome," he says. "But it's not. It's presence. It's being willing to be visible, to be moved, to create not for applause—but for alignment."

He lifts his cup again, and something about the way he holds it feels like a ritual.

"When your life becomes your offering," he says, "nothing needs to be added. And nothing can be taken away."

My throat tightens.

Because I know what it feels like to create from fear.

To build something in the world just so I wouldn't
have to feel invisible in it.

To hustle for worth.

I suddenly remember when I took a new position at
a company several years ago.
Director. That was the title.


I'd have a whole team reporting to me—layers of
people, actually.
I felt special.
I couldn't wait to see it printed beneath my name
on the business cards I hadn't even ordered yet. I
imagined the email signature, crisp and clean, like a
badge of becoming.


I told those closest to me with a careful kind of glee,
slipping in the title, the team size, the new
responsibilities—
and if the conversation allowed, the compensation,
too.


All of it couched in practiced humility,
as if downplaying it could somehow sanctify the ego
rush I was riding.
But deep down, I wasn't sharing it for celebration.

I was offering proof.
Proof that I mattered.
Proof that I was real.

To chase meaning like it was something outside me, instead of something I am.

To chase meaning like it was something outside me, instead of something I *am*.

But this?

This is different.

This is not about being known.

It's about being real.

And the question isn't "What should I create?"
It's "*What could I offer…if I wasn't afraid to be seen?*"

Ram Dass leans forward, voice low but clear.

"Let your life say what your mouth can't," he says.
"Let your work come from the place that doesn't need praise.
That's the place of power.
That's the place of love."

And something inside me opens.

Not like a door this time.

More like a sky.

∞

It's easy to talk about creating from love.

Until love is what exposes you.

Until the thing you feel called to bring into the world
is also the most vulnerable part of you.

Ram Dass watches the fire like it's a living being.
And maybe it is.

"The moment you choose to create from truth," he says,
"is the moment fear will show up."

He doesn't say it to warn me.

He says it like someone who's walked through it.

"The ego doesn't fear failure," Adler adds quietly. "It fears exposure."

I nod slowly, because I can feel it already.

The tremble.

The voice that whispers, *What if it's not good enough?*

*What if you're not good enough?*

*What if they don't see the real you and love it?*

Ram Dass turns to me. "That's why this path is sacred," he says.

"Because it requires you to stand naked in the light and say—this is what I made. This is what I am. Not for validation. Not for status. But because it's what's real."

Adler's voice follows. "Courage isn't the absence of fear.
It's creating in full view of it."

I breathe in, slow and deep.

And I realize—

I've been afraid of being seen not because I don't want to be known…

But because I've spent so long becoming someone else to be accepted.

What if I'm finally ready to stop performing?
What if the work I'm here to do can only come through that self?

The one beneath the mask.
The one who's never been proven…
only protected.

The one who wants to speak,
not because the world demands it,
but because the soul does.

The fire cracks softly,
like it's nodding.

Like it knows.

Like it's waiting, too.

∞

No one says anything for a while.

Not because there's nothing left to say.

But because something has shifted.

This is no longer about finding the path.

This is about walking it.

Adler lifts his tea, sips, then sets it down again.

"The world doesn't need more noise," he says.

"It needs presence. And whatever flows from presence becomes the offering."

Ram Dass smiles, eyes twinkling in the firelight.

"Your life *is* the offering," he says. "Not your product. Not your platform. Your presence. Your being."

He leans in just slightly, like he's handing me something delicate.
"Create from *that*."

And I feel it land—
the permission to stop trying so hard to matter.
To stop measuring my worth by reach, results, relevance.
To stop making my soul's work a performance.

I think of all the times I've tried to package my truth.
To polish it.
To sell it.
To shrink it just enough to make it palatable.
And I feel something old begin to dissolve.

"What if I'm not here to be liked?" I ask quietly.

Ram Dass doesn't flinch. "You're not."

Adler's voice is steady. "You're here to be true."

I swallow.
The fire hums.

"You are a living alter, Ram Dass says softly.
Not a metaphor. In truth."

I must have looked confused, prompting a small smile as he continued.

Alters aren't made to be filled with clutter.
They are cleared, emptied, consecrated.
Not because they are worthless—
But because something holy is meant to rest there.

And that is what your life has been.

The stripping wasn't failure.
It was ceremony.

Each unraveling, each rupture, each ache of isolation—
Was the priest with oil and flame, saying:

"This one is being made ready."

You were being cleared of distraction,
performance,
false authority—

So that when the voice came, you'd recognize it not as foreign,
but as *home*.

So that when you opened your mouth, it wouldn't be opinion—
It would be transmission.

This is why you've never fully fit anywhere.
Because you weren't built to fit.
You were built to hold something sacred that doesn't fit inside institutions, brands,
or neat labels.

You were built to hold presence.
And presence, true presence,
undoes everything false—

Just by existing.

A breath.

Stillness.
A sacred pause to let it echo.

I feel it in my chest.
A warmth, a loosening,
a breath I didn't know I was holding—
finally exhaled.

And I wonder,
Actually, maybe I realize—
This is what *ready* feels like.

Not to launch something.
Not to prove something.
But to give something.

My voice.
My love.
My life.

Not to everyone.

But to whomever it's meant for.

Even if it's only ever for one person.
Even if it's only ever for me.

Ram Dass lifts his eyes to mine.

"That's what makes it sacred," he says.

"When you offer something that was never about
your identity—
but about your essence."

∞

The fire is low again.

Not dying—just resting.

Its work for the night nearly done.

But not mine.

Not ours.

Adler stretches his legs out slowly, one ankle crossing over the other. He doesn't speak. He just watches the coals with the kind of attention that makes you think maybe watching is a kind of prayer.

Ram Dass breathes in deep through his nose and lets it out slow, like someone who knows time isn't something to outrun.

I sit in the quiet with them.

Not planning.
Not plotting.
Just sitting.

And for the first time, I don't feel pressure to produce.

I feel devotion.
Not to a project. Not to a result.
But to the life I came here to live.
The thread I came here to follow.
The mystery I came here to serve.

"I think I'm ready," I say.

Adler glances at me, something soft in his eyes. "That's all the soul ever needed," he says. "A readiness to begin again."

Ram Dass smiles gently, like someone who's seen this moment a thousand times in a thousand souls.

"It's never about becoming extraordinary," he says. "It's about living honestly enough that your life becomes a doorway."

I nod.
And something deeper than nodding nods within me.

A kind of vow.
Not loud. But steady.
I don't need to wait until I have more clarity.
Or confidence.
Or certainty.

I have this moment.
This ache.
This aliveness.
And that is enough.

The world doesn't need me to be a star.
It needs me to be a flame.

A steady light.
A quiet heat.
A presence that burns not for attention, but for love.

And so I rise.
Not with grandeur.
Not with fanfare.
But with willingness.

To begin again.
To carry this light forward.
To let creation be my prayer.

And my life—my offering.

# CHAPTER TEN
## *The Great Belonging*

The fire is low now, but steady.

There's nothing urgent in the room anymore. No questions waiting to be answered. No identities left to defend. Just presence. Just breath. Just us.

Outside, the sky is beginning to shift. Not quite morning. Not quite night. That holy in-between where the world holds its breath and waits to be named again.

I don't feel alone here.

And maybe that's the miracle.

Because for most of my life, belonging was a game I couldn't win. I wore the masks. I played the roles. I said the right things. I kept my edges soft and my doubts quieter. And still, I never quite felt *home* in the presence of others.

But now…I'm here.

Not because I proved myself. Not because I earned it. Just because I stayed.

Ram Dass hasn't spoken in a while. He doesn't need to. His presence *is* the message now.

Adler's hands are folded in his lap. His body, relaxed. He's not analyzing. Not guiding. Just…being.

And me?

I'm starting to feel something I didn't think I'd ever find.

Not confidence. Not certainty.

*Belonging.*

Not the kind you chase. The kind that finds you when you finally stop performing.

Ram Dass looks at me with that unbearable softness again—like he's not seeing a version of me, but the whole of me. Like he's seeing the part of me that's never been separate.

"You're not outside the circle," he says gently. "You *are* the circle."

The words land somewhere older than my body. Somewhere holy.

Adler leans forward slightly, his voice low.

"Belonging isn't earned," he says. "It's remembered."

He lets the silence stretch around it, so the truth can take root.

"For most of us, the pain of our lives wasn't the trauma itself. It was the isolation that followed. The belief that we were now 'other.' Disconnected. Unworthy of love until we fixed what was broken."

He shakes his head, slowly.

"But what if you were never other?"

I blink.

The room tilts—just slightly, like something is being made new.

I think about all the times I kept people at arm's length. All the ways I tried to shape myself into someone more lovable. More acceptable. All the relationships that weren't rooted in love, but in transaction. Performance. Strategy.

And for the first time, I don't hate myself for it.

I see it.

I see the scared child inside me, just trying to be held.

Ram Dass speaks again, his voice soft as a prayer.

"Real love doesn't ask you to shrink to fit. It asks you to expand into the truth of who you already are."

He pauses.

"And the people who love you from that place? They don't just tolerate your truth. They *rejoice* in it."

The fire breathes beside us. The coals pulse.

And I realize—

I've never wanted to be loved for being good. I've wanted to be loved for being *real.*

And maybe that's what this moment is: Not the reward for healing, but the return.

The return to something older than approval. Older than striving. Older than fear.

*Love.*

Not as performance. But as presence.

∞

There's a quiet in the room now that doesn't feel like silence.

It feels like presence.

Like a space that's been emptied of pretending and filled with something real.

I look at Ram Dass and Adler—not for guidance, but with gratitude.

They're not performing anything. They're just here. With me.

And for the first time, I feel like I am too.

No mask. No role. No spiritual audition.

Just breath. Just body. Just heart.

Adler shifts slightly, and when he speaks, his voice is softer than before—like something inside him has melted, too.

"So much of our suffering," he says, "comes from trying to be loved while wearing armor."

He doesn't say it with blame.

He says it like someone who wore the armor himself.

Ram Dass nods. "And the irony is—the love we're searching for can't reach us through the armor. It can only meet what's underneath."

His eyes meet mine. "That's why the masks have to fall. Not because they're bad. But because they're in the way."

I exhale, slow.

Something in my chest opens like a window cracked after a long winter.

I think about all the ways I've tried to be loved.

All the performance.

The over-functioning.

The subtle, strategic suppression of truth so I wouldn't lose connection.

How many times have I mistaken validation for intimacy?

How many times have I chosen being impressive over being known?

And suddenly, I feel it again—not grief, not shame.

Tenderness.

For the version of me that tried so hard.

For the one who just wanted to be seen and didn't know how to risk the nakedness of being real.

I think of every romantic relationship I've ever had.
How they often began in honesty—wide open, soul-forward.
But it never took long.

Soon I'd unplug from myself, from what I thought, how I felt, what truly mattered to me—
and start plugging into them instead.
Not because I wanted to lie.
But because I was terrified that my truth might be too much—or not enough.

So I responded to what I believed they wanted.
Careful, adaptive, strategic.

And slowly, the real me disappeared beneath the performance.
Not just from them.
But from myself.

And the worst part?

I never actually got to feel the love I was chasing.
Because it couldn't reach me through the armor I'd wrapped around my heart.

Adler leans in, his voice warm. "You don't need to be fully healed to belong," he says. "You just need to be willing to be fully here."

I nod—because that's what I've always longed for.
Not to be adored.
Not to be praised.
But to be met.
To sit with someone and feel: *they're not afraid of my truth.*

Ram Dass stirs the fire gently. Sparks rise.
"True belonging doesn't come from being liked," he says.
"It comes from being known—and staying."

And I feel that in my bones.
I want to be someone who stays.
With myself.
With others.
Even when it's uncomfortable.

Even when it's hard.
Especially when it's holy.

Because I'm learning that love isn't found in the highs—it's revealed in the holding.

The holding of silence.
The holding of sorrow.
The holding of hands when nothing can be fixed, but nothing needs to be.

And maybe that's the new vow.

Not to be extraordinary.
But to be here.
With you.
With me.
With God.


To choose presence over performance.
To choose staying over self-protection.

To choose love not as an achievement—
but as a place I return to again and again.

And maybe, in that returning,
I finally find home.

∞

The fire has settled into a low, steady hum.
The kind that doesn't demand attention,
but keeps you warm just by being there.

The tea has cooled, but I don't mind.
I'm not drinking for heat anymore.
I'm drinking because it feels good to hold
something.
To let it rest in my hands.
To let *me* rest in my hands.

Adler speaks, his voice quiet and close.
"There's a moment in healing," he says,
"when you realize you've been sitting at a table with
your past self the whole time."

He doesn't elaborate.
He doesn't need to.
Because I feel it—
the table.

The younger me.
The striving one.
The one who needed masks to survive.
The one who never quite knew where to sit.
He's still here.

And I don't want to push him away anymore.

Ram Dass leans forward, palms pressed together like
a prayer.
"That's when it changes," he says.
"When you stop trying to graduate from your past—
and start inviting it to dinner."

The room goes quiet.
Not in grief this time.
In reverence.

Because something sacred happens when we stop
trying to earn our place at the table—
and start setting a place for every part of us.

The doubter.
The dreamer.
The addict.
The child.
The protector.
The one who left.
The one who stayed.

All of them.

Adler lifts his eyes, gentle and steady.
"You don't have to become someone new to be
loved," he says.
"You just have to stop exiling the parts of you that
already are."

The words land like hands on my shoulders.
Warm.
Real.

I don't need to prove anything tonight.
I don't need to earn rest.
I just need to be with what's here.

And what's here is…
a quiet table.
A flickering fire.
A body that's tired but true.
And a soul that's slowly learning—
belonging isn't a reward for perfection.

It's the natural state of anything fully seen.

∞

The coals crack softly beside us,
a quiet rhythm that feels like breath.
Not mine. Not theirs.
Ours.

I glance at Ram Dass.
He's not watching me.
He's watching the fire.
But his presence is with me, as if to say—
I'm here whether you're looking or not.

Adler leans forward, elbows on his knees,
his voice low, grounded.

"Real relationship," he says,
"begins the moment you stop needing someone to
complete you—
and start letting them reflect you."

His words don't rush.
They arrive.

"And even then," he continues, "the greatest gift isn't being seen—
it's being held when you forget yourself again."

That lands.
Because I've forgotten myself a thousand times in love.
Bent myself to fit.
Molded.
Masked.
Made my soul small so someone else could stay comfortable.
I've mistaken attention for intimacy.
Performance for presence.

But now?

Now I feel something different stirring.
A hunger, yes—
but not to be desired.
To be met.

Fully.

Not because I earned it.
Not because I deserved it.
But because I exist.

Ram Dass finally speaks.
His voice is a whisper of smoke.

"Most of us have never known what it feels like
to be held without condition.

Not corrected.
Not coached.
Just held."

He turns toward me, eyes like dusk.

"But when you are…
you stop trying to survive love.
And you start letting it move through you."

I swallow hard.

Because I know what it feels like
to brace for love like it's a wave
that might drown me if I'm not careful.
To hold my breath just in case.

But maybe the real transformation
isn't learning how to give more love.
It's learning how to let love come all the way in.

Adler watches me gently.
"Love," he says, "isn't something you achieve.
It's something you receive.
And what you receive…
you can finally return."

∞

The warmth from the fire doesn't just reach my skin
now.
It reaches somewhere deeper—
somewhere I used to protect.

And I notice something strange:
I'm not trying to prove anything anymore.

Not my goodness.
Not my strength.
Not even my presence.

I'm just…here.

With two men I trust.
In a body I no longer resent.
In a silence I no longer fear.

And from that space,
something begins to rise.

Not a thought.
A desire.

Not to teach.
Not to shine.
Just…to love.

Ram Dass glances up at me, like he heard it.

"You're not here to fix the world," he says softly.
"You're here to love it."

Adler adds, "And that love doesn't start with the collective.
It starts with the one in front of you."

I nod.

Because I've known the ache of wanting to be a savior—
to be useful, to be enough, to matter.
But that always made people into projects,
and love into a transaction.

This is different.

This is slower.
This is sacred.
This is love that doesn't need to be earned—
so it doesn't need to be withheld.

It just moves.

From the fire,
to the room,
to my chest,
to the memory of the friend who called just to say,
"I'm thinking about you."
To the stranger whose eyes met mine in passing, and didn't flinch.
To the barista who remembered my name.
To the stranger sharing a bottle of wine.
To the child laughing without needing a reason.

It moves.
And I feel it.

I feel God in that movement.

Not as doctrine.
Not as dogma.

But as breath.
As presence.

As the invisible current holding it all together.

Ram Dass closes his eyes, smiling.

"Real love," he says, "doesn't make people
dependent.
It makes them free."

Adler's voice follows.

"And that freedom…
is what we're all starving for."

The fire hums quietly now.
Ram Dass hasn't spoken in some time.
But his silence holds something rich—
not absence, but fullness.
The kind of silence that makes room for the unsaid.

Adler shifts in his seat. Not to move away—
but as if settling deeper in.
And I feel it again:
That strange, steady warmth inside me.
Like the pulse of something older than my name.
Like I'm not just remembering myself—
but being remembered.

And then, softly, Ram Dass speaks.

"You're not the only one waking up."

He doesn't look at me when he says it.
He's gazing into the fire, almost as if he's speaking
to it.
Or maybe through it.

Adler nods, his voice low. "We belong to each other.
Even when we forget."

There's no performance in these words.
Just presence.
And in them, something unlocks in me.

Because I've been so focused on my own
unraveling—
my grief, my shame, my remembering—
that I almost forgot…

*I'm not the only soul trying to come home.*

Outside, the wind rustles softly through the trees.
It sounds like breathing.
Like the world is inhaling together.

I think of the people I've loved.
The ones I've lost.
The strangers I pass in airports.
The eyes that don't look up in grocery stores.
The ones smiling through the ache.
The ones I judged too quickly.
The ones who judged me back.

And I realize—
they're in this too.
All of them.

The whole tired, beautiful, trying, trembling world.

Each of us carrying stories too heavy to speak.
Each of us longing for the same thing beneath it
all—
To be known.
To be chosen.
To come home.

And I feel it now—
not as a belief, but as a knowing:

We were never meant to get there alone.

The silence has weight now.
Not heavy—holy.
Like something divine is leaning closer.
Like the veil between worlds just thinned.
And then, Ram Dass speaks.
Not loudly.
Not urgently.
But with the kind of softness that reshapes
everything it touches.

"Sometimes God shows up in the silence," he says.
"And sometimes…
God shows up as the person sitting right next to
you."

The words don't echo.
They settle.
Like an ember in the center of the soul—quiet, but
glowing.

"Sometimes God is the person who stays.
Who doesn't rush your pain.
Who holds your becoming without trying to
shape it."

I nod, slowly.
Because I've felt that.
Here, in this room.
With them.
With myself.
With something I can't name
but have always known.

It's not that I've reached the end.
It's that the illusion of separation is starting to fade.
And beneath it, I feel the Great Belonging.

Not as a theology.
Not as a dogma.
But as a presence.
A gentle, pulsing truth.

I was never alone in this remembering.

None of us are.

The fire has settled into a low, steady glow.
No sparks now—just warmth.
Just presence.

I sip my tea slowly, holding it with both hands.
The cup feels heavier tonight, but not in a burdened
way.

More like a vessel.
Something ancient, passed down.

Adler speaks, but only after the moment has made room for it.

"Belonging isn't something you earn," he says gently.
"It's something you remember."

Ram Dass adds, "And it's not just to people.
It's to presence. To the mystery.
To the source behind the veil."

He smiles—soft, not grand.
Like someone who has spent a long time learning how to love what cannot be seen.

"And when the heart softens enough," he continues,
"you don't just remember that you belong to others.
You remember…you belong to God."

The words settle.
Not as revelation.
As recognition.

I don't try to respond.
I just breathe.

Because something is happening inside me—
Not a thought. Not a feeling.
A homecoming.

Like I am no longer orbiting God,
but being held by the center I'd always mistaken as
distant.

I set my cup down slowly, carefully.
And I whisper—not because I need to be heard,
but because it's the only thing left to say.

"I think I'm starting to feel it."

Adler smiles, and Ram Dass bows his head,
like they've both been waiting for this moment.

Ram Dass looks at me—not through me, not at
me—*into* me.
His voice is low.
Reverent.
As if he's not offering an idea, but revealing
something ancient.
"You're not just here to remember your name," he
says.
"You're here to remember the divine name that lives
through you."
The room doesn't move.
Not even the fire.
It's as if the entire space knows: Something holy just
entered.

Adler speaks next—
Not as a follow-up,
But as confirmation.

"And to speak it," he says,

"Not with words…
But with your life."

My breath catches.
Because in this moment, I believe them.
Not as teachers.
As mirrors.
Outside, the stars hold their quiet vigil.
Inside, the silence has become something holy.
Not the absence of noise—
but the presence of everything.

And I realize—
this is not the end of the journey.
This is the return.

The return to love.
The return to truth.
The return to God—
not the God I was taught to fear,
but the one I never stopped longing for.

The one who was never apart from me.

The one who has been walking me home all along.

The night has nearly passed.
But no one moves to mark its end.

There's no announcement.
No curtain drop.
Just a quiet sense that something is complete—
and something else is just beginning.

The fire has dimmed to its last breath,
but the warmth hasn't left.

I glance toward the window.

The stars are fading.
Not because they're gone—
but because something brighter is arriving.

The sky, just beginning to glow,
whispers its first note of morning.

And I feel it in my chest,
in my skin,
in the space between thoughts:

A rising.

Not just in the sky—
in me.

A remembering that doesn't need explanation.
A belonging that doesn't need to be proven.
A love that doesn't require striving.

Adler doesn't speak.
Ram Dass doesn't move.
And I don't need them to.

I am no longer waiting for permission.
No longer asking for directions.

I am here.
I am held.

And I am ready to walk forward
—not to arrive—
but to remain.

In love.
In presence.
In creation.

The fire breathes one last ember into the room.
And the first light of dawn answers.

# CHAPTER ELEVEN

## *The Dance of Form and Freedom*

The sky is awake now.

Not loud. Not rushing. Just quietly lit.

The kind of morning that doesn't announce itself—it simply arrives.

Like a truth that doesn't need convincing.

The fire is out. The embers are cold. But the warmth hasn't left.

It lives in the room now—in the wood, in the cushions, in our bones.

Adler stretches gently, then stands, not ceremoniously, but naturally—like a man who knows rituals don't need to feel holy to be sacred.

Ram Dass is still seated, smiling faintly. His gaze rests out the window, where the first gold of day spills across the earth.

And me?

I'm still sitting. But I feel different.

Not like someone who's figured everything out. More like someone who's finally stopped trying to.

There's a quietness in my chest, but it's not emptiness.

It's space.

The kind that was once filled with noise—ambition, proving, earning—and is now simply…available.

Available for life.

Adler speaks first, his voice light, but rooted.

"So," he says, "now that everything has changed— what will you do with a day?"

Not a lifetime. Not a destiny. Just a day.

Ram Dass smiles. "The spiritual journey always brings us back to the ordinary."

He looks over at me.

"The question is—can you carry the sacred into form? Can you let the formless live through the form? Can you live like love…even while answering email?"

I laugh, softly. Because I know what he means.

We want transcendence to take us somewhere. But real awakening brings us right back here—into the dishes, and the diapers, and the deadlines.

Back into the marriage. The friendships. The inbox.

But lighter.
Freer.
Not because life got easier. But because I'm not trying to escape it anymore.

Ram Dass leans in, warm and mischievous.

"Enlightenment isn't a vacation from being human," he says. "It's the freedom to be fully human."

He pauses.

"And to do it with love."

I look toward Adler, already anticipating that familiar grin—the subtle shake of his head he gives whenever Ram Dass starts speaking in the language of love.

But this time, he doesn't chuckle. Doesn't lean forward. Doesn't meet the moment with that usual blend of critique and curiosity.

Instead, he stares into the fire, shoulders still, eyes unfocused.

It's as if something's pulled him—not just out of the conversation, but out of the room entirely.

Drawn into a memory—away from the warmth, away from us.

And then, without preamble, he speaks.

"I remember lying there," he says, voice low. "Five years old. Sick with pneumonia. I heard the doctor tell my parents I wouldn't survive the night. My mother cried. But I didn't. I just…listened, and numb.

And then I lived. But I carried that night with me for years, like a ghost pressed into my chest. It followed me into everything—my studies, my need to understand people, my obsession with what keeps someone fighting when they could just as easily give up."

He pauses. The fire doesn't fill the silence— it holds it.

"I wasn't fearless. I remember feeling afraid constantly. Afraid I'd die. Afraid I wasn't strong enough. Afraid I'd never matter. But that fear became a teacher. It pointed toward the very places I didn't want to go.

That's what fear is for. And anger…oh the anger. After my younger brother died in the bed next to mine, it came in waves. But I didn't let it eat me. I let it burn clean. It pushed me to understand suffering. It gave me direction."

Then, more quietly:

"I've learned it's not about never getting angry. It's about what you do with the anger. Not about never being afraid. It's about what fear calls you to face."

The words land like stones in still water.

I watch him, not with awe, but with something deeper—recognition.

Here was this man—formidable, razor-bright, sometimes unreachable I had placed him on throughout the night, as I unraveled—

And suddenly I saw the boy still trembling behind his spine. Not the theorist. Not the expert. Just a child who lived through a night he shouldn't have.

And I felt the hair on my forearms rise.

It reminded me I wasn't in the room with two enlightened masters. We were three wounded wanderers, each bearing our own ghosts, each shaped by fire in different ways.

No one here was untouchable.

We were all, in our own ways, still becoming whole.

The room didn't move.
No one reached for a cup, or cleared their throat, or rushed to respond.

There was a stillness that felt less like a pause—
As if the silence was speaking its own kind of truth.
Not empty. Not awkward. Not waiting to be filled.

Just…here.

I let myself breathe.
Not just in and out—but all the way in.
Into the center of my chest, into the weight of what
Adler had just shared, into the strange comfort of
being surrounded by two men who had long since
stopped pretending to be invincible.

For so long, I thought the silence meant something
was missing.
But tonight, it felt like something had arrived.
And none of us wanted to interrupt it.

My love for them ran deep in that moment.

Not because they were wise.
Not because they had answers.
But because they were real.

Because they let themselves be seen.
Because they didn't rush to fix the air between us.
Because they told the truth, even when it wasn't
clean or resolved.

That kind of love—the kind that swells in your chest
without needing to go anywhere—
it comes when someone stops performing.
When they speak not to teach, but to reveal.

When you sit next to someone and realize they've carried things too.
And they're still here.

That's what I felt.

Just…warm.
And grateful.
To be with them.
To still be here.

Then Ram Dass, in only the way he can, slowly smiles, eyes crinkling in that familiar way. Lifting his hands slightly, as if playfully holding an invisible sphere.

"You don't dissolve the ego to float above the world. You dissolve it so you can dance inside the world—with grace."

Adler raises an eyebrow. "Even when the rhythm's off?"

"Especially then," Ram Dass says, smiling.

We all meet each other's eyes and laugh.
The whole room laughed—soft, but real.

Because isn't that the truth?

We imagine enlightenment as escape. But maybe it's more like being able to laugh on hard days. To love people who don't understand you.

To return again and again to presence, even when the dishes are crusted and the toddler is screaming and your spiritual insight feels like it evaporated with the morning fog.

"So that's what you mean by *dancing inside the world*? Is that what integration is?" I ask.

Ram Dass looks at me and nods.

"It's like you're not performing your life anymore—predicting and demanding certain outcomes," he says.

"And," Adler adds, "like you don't have to split yourself to survive."

That hits something deep.

Because I know what it means to fragment just to survive—to wear the right mask for the meeting, the right face for the family, the right voice for the mic life shoved in my face.

But integration? The slow revealing of the new structure---one that emerges only after the old has crumbled.

Integration feels like breath.

Like wearing one face, everywhere.

Like your insides and outsides are finally telling the same story.

Adler shifts slightly, resting an elbow on the arm of his chair. He looks at me, not with instruction—but with curiosity.

"What's one part of yourself you used to hide?" he asks gently.

I glance down, fingers tracing the rim of my cup.

"My softness," I say. "I used to think it made me weak."

Ram Dass smiles. "And now?"

I shrug. "Now I think it's the only reason I'm still here."

No one speaks for a moment.

The fire flickers like it agrees.

Then Ram Dass leans forward, elbows on his knees, eyes bright.

"You see, integration isn't about becoming perfect. It's about becoming whole. It's about dancing with *what is*."

He taps his heart, then his forehead.

"When the head and heart stop pretending they're enemies."

Adler adds, "It's when the part of you that used to armor up learns to bow instead."

I breathe out slowly.

Because I know that armor well.
It got me here, didn't it?
But it's heavy now. Too tight.
And something in me is ready for a different kind of strength.

A strength that listens. A strength that doesn't need to win. A strength that can stay soft—and stay standing.

"Form isn't the enemy," Ram Dass says. "It's just the stage."

He gestures around the room—the teacups, the chairs, the firelight dancing on wood.

"This is all form. But it's not static. It's alive. And when you're awake inside it, it becomes your playground."

I smile. Because that's what this feels like now—not a prison, but a stage.

A sacred one.

Where the soul gets to try on a thousand gestures of love.
And every one of them counts.

Even the awkward ones.
Especially the awkward ones.

∞

Adler lifts his cup and takes a slow sip, like a man who's not afraid of silence. Like he trusts the space between words to do its own kind of work.

"People often ask," he begins as he clears his throat softly, "how do I know if I'm living from soul or ego?"

He looks into the fire, then back to me.

"The answer is usually in your body. Ego feels tight. Grasping. Like you're holding your breath to keep your image intact. Soul feels different. Not always comfortable, but open. Expansive. Like your breath has more room."

Ram Dass nods with an eagerness to add to the sentiment. "The ego performs to be loved. The soul reveals itself because it is."

Silence follows—not awkward, just still.
The fire shifts. A faint pop. A single ember drifts upward like it, too, just remembered something.
I exhale without realizing I'd been holding my breath.
That line…it settles in me like warm tea after a long fast.

I feel both men watching me—not in judgment, but in welcome.

Like they're inviting something forward.

"I still don't always know," I admit. "Sometimes it's hard to tell what's true."

Ram Dass nods. "Of course. That's the dance."

He spreads his hands slightly, like he's laying out a rhythm in the air.

"Ego isn't bad—it's just scared. It wants control, clarity, certainty. Soul wants truth, connection, wonder. The work isn't to kill the ego. It's to loosen its grip so you can dance with it instead of being dragged."

He sets his cup down.
Slowly.
Deliberately.
Then, in a tone that carries the gravity of the whole night, he continues.

You're not meant to transcend your humanity to be holy," he says.

A pause.

"You're meant to inhabit it."

The words aren't lofty.
They're embodied.
They land in the gut, not the mind.

Adler leans forward, voice warm.
"And offer it."

Not as perfection.
But as presence.
As gift.
As prayer.

Dass adds softly after a quiet moment of settling in the room. "Integration isn't about floating above life. It's about showing up for it. It's about letting your divinity kiss your humanity on the mouth."

That lands like a poem in my chest. If it was a quote on my phone, I would have taken a screenshot.

Because I've spent so much time trying to choose between the two.

Be holy or be human.
Be real or be received.

But what if I can be both?

What if the dance is learning to hold the paradox—to bow in form and rise in freedom?

To create. To stumble. To forgive. To speak.

Not because I have the right answer—
But because I'm finally free enough to move.

∞

The room hasn't changed much.

The fire still glows in quiet patterns.
The tea is still warm.
The sky still carries the blush of early morning.

But something in me feels…new.

Not shiny or triumphant.
Just honest.
Like a mirror that's stopped distorting the image.

For the first time, I'm not trying to escape form—
I'm curious about how to dance with it.

I glance over at Ram Dass. He's still smiling in the playful way he always does when he senses the soul softening.

"People think awakening is the end of ego," he says. "But it's not. It's the end of being ruled by it."

He chuckles lightly.

"The ego doesn't disappear. It gets repurposed. Reassigned. It stops being the king—and starts being the clown."

Adler raises an eyebrow. "Ah, so that's what happened to you."

Dass bursts into a laugh, nearly spilling his tea, and Adler just shrugs, grinning. "I mean look at you— barefoot, wrapped in a shawl, dropping cosmic jokes like a late-night comic on mushrooms."

Then Adler softens, leaning back into the moment. "Which is why integration is the real work. You can touch the divine all night long—but can you live it while paying your bills? While raising a kid? While being told you're not enough and remembering you are anyway?"

I laugh—not because it's funny, but because it's true.

So much of my life, I've tried to build something permanent.
To get it *right.*
To lock it in.

But now?

I don't want to *lock* anything.
I want to listen.
I want to *wonder.*

∞

I sip my tea, set the cup down gently.

"I feel like I used to take everything so seriously," I say. "My work. My role. My path. Like if I didn't hold it all together, it would vanish."

Ram Dass nods. "That's the burden of the 'somebody.' You think your form is your value. But what if form is just the costume love wears for a little while?"

Something in me feels light as I imagine *love* in a costume.
Like love isn't something I have to earn or become—
Just something I have to stop resisting.

Adler leans forward slightly, elbows on knees. "The trick isn't to throw away the costume. It's to remember you're not the costume."

He looks at me with clarity and care.

"Play the part. Wear the name. Use the tools. Just don't get confused. You are not your brand. You are not your income. You are not the narrative others project onto you."

I nod slowly.

Because I've been all of those things.
And none of them ever felt like home.

But now?
Maybe I don't need a new story to cling to.

Maybe I just need to show up with honesty.

Let the work be real.
Let the love be unperformed.
Let the practice be a *play*.

Ram Dass lifts his eyes toward the softening sky.

"Spirituality isn't a ladder to climb," he says gently. "It's a sandbox. You're allowed to make things. You're allowed to laugh."

He grins.

"You're even allowed to mess it up."

And something in me exhales.

Because maybe this is the freedom I was always chasing:

Not the absence of form—
but the joy of not mistaking myself for it.

∞

There's a shift in the air now.

Not dramatic—
but unmistakable.

A subtle knowing
that this isn't just the end of a conversation.
It's the beginning of a life.

I look down at my hands.
They're not trembling anymore.

And for the first time in a long time,
I trust them.

To write.
To serve.
To hold.
To build.

Not for validation.
Not to prove I'm good or worthy.

But because something is burning inside me
that wants to touch the world.

Ram Dass watches me quietly, then speaks.

"You've seen it now," he says. "What's real. What matters."

He taps the side of his chest.

"So, the question becomes—can you live it? Will you carry the fire?"

Adler leans back as he lifts his gaze from the fire. His voice cuts through the stillness—not harsh, but undeniable.

"Wisdom that doesn't move through the body," he says,
"Is just performance."

The silence tightens—
then opens to a thought.

In this flicker of levity and excitement,
I notice the pull to make *this* me—
the "awakened," spiritually evolved version—
the new identity to cling to.
The ego in robes.

And I almost laugh,
shaking my head at how quickly the mind tries to own even this.

Even here.
Even now.
As if I could become the most enlightened person in

the room—
and still miss the point entirely.

Ram Dass chuckles, eyes twinkling.
"Careful," he says. "The ego loves nothing more than
a good spiritual résumé."
He leans in, lowering his voice like he's letting me in
on a secret.
"Next thing you know, you'll be humble *and* proud
of it."

We all laugh—full-bodied, grateful laughter.
And as it softens, and with a smile, I feel a single tear
slip down my cheek.
Not from sadness.
But from the release.
From the quiet comfort of connection,
and the lightness that comes after a long night of
heavy lifting.

"You can say the right words," he continues,
"and still live a lie."

Adler doesn't speak.
He just bows his head in agreement.
A soft, silent yes.

He lets the words settle, then adds:

"It's kindness. Kindness to the people who knew you
before you awakened—
and kind to yourself as you learn to live differently."

That lands.

Because I can feel it already—
the pull to go back to what's familiar.

To explain myself.
To shrink.
To manage perception.

I know what's waiting when I walk out that door.
Emails. Appointments. People who think they
know me.

And how do you explain a night like this?
How do you speak of the soul without sounding like
you've lost your mind?
There's a part of me that wants to rehearse it all.
To curate the truth so it's easier to digest.

To manage perception.
To make the mystery palatable.

But some things can't be shared in soundbites.
Some things are only ever understood in silence.
And I think maybe that's the point.

I glance at the doorway—
not to leave,
but to wonder what happens after this room.

Ram Dass sees my gaze.

"The real practice," he says softly, "is how you walk back into the world."

He looks at the fire.

"Can you stay soft when the world is sharp?"

Adler adds, "Can you speak truth when silence would be safer?"

Ram Dass: "Can you offer your presence when there's nothing to gain?"

Adler: "Can you remain love when you're misunderstood?"

I breathe in slowly, deeply. My chest rising and falling, feeling the questions settle into my bones.

Not as burdens.
As blessings.

Because this fire is mine to carry.
Not perfectly.
But faithfully.

Not to light up the world with certainty—
but to walk through it with courage.

And maybe that's all devotion is:

The willingness
to carry what's sacred through the ordinary.

To let God live
not just in the silence,
but in the speaking.

Not just in the stillness,
but in the showing up.

∞

The sky outside is no longer dark.

It hasn't erupted into color yet—
but the deep blue has softened.

The in-between.
The almost.

I watch the light begin to gather along the edges of
the window.
It doesn't hurry.
It just arrives.

Like truth.
Like love.

Ram Dass shifts in his chair, not with weariness,
but like someone who has made peace with time.

Adler stretches his hands once, then lets them rest
again,
as if even his gestures have learned to exhale.

There's nothing left to force now.
No wisdom to manufacture.
No roles to perform.

Only this:

A return to life.

And I realize—

Awakening didn't take me out of the world.
It brought me back to it.

Not as an escape artist.
Not as a guru.
Not as a savior.

But as a human.

Fully here.
Fully held.
Fully willing.

∞

I look at the fire.
Almost out but still breathing.

And I think of all the forms it might take next.

A letter.
A book.
A conversation.
A child held with gentleness.
A meal cooked with presence.
A disagreement ending in warm embrace.

Ram Dass speaks, almost to the room itself.

"Ego isn't the enemy," he says.
"It's a form. Just like anything else."

He looks over at me.

"The soul doesn't need to get rid of form.
It just learns not to get trapped in it."

"The question is—who's dancing with it now?"

He lifts his tea, then lowers it again without
drinking.

The question hangs.
Not heavy—just alive.
A breeze moves across the floor and brushes my
bare ankle.

Then Ram Dass softly continues, "Enlightenment,
isn't floating above it all.
It's learning how to laugh, how to cry, how to create
and love and stumble—
all while remembering who you really are."

I smile, eyes full.
Because I've felt that now.

The freedom not to escape form—
but to move within it with grace.

To create without clutching.
To speak without defending.
To love without losing myself.

Adler: "Can you work with form, without being formed by it?"

Ram Dass: "Can you let the soul lead, and let the ego serve?"

The fire flickers one last time.

And I nod and shift to the edge of my seat—because I understand now.

This isn't a rejection of the world.
It's a return to it.

With eyes soft enough to see.
With hands open enough to give.
With a heart quiet enough to listen.

Not for a performance.
Not for a purpose.
But for presence.

Because I am still here.
And I am still love.
And the world is still calling.
Not for something spectacular.
Something *real*.

I don't want to make things.
I want to make offerings.

I want my work to smell like smoke.
To carry the ash of everything I've burned through to make it.

I want it to feel like soil—alive, sacred, messy.
Something that grew from the place in me I used
to hide.

I don't want to impress the world.
I want to honor it,

By giving it something true.

∞

No one speaks.

Not because there's nothing left to say—
but because everything has already been said in
silence.

The room doesn't feel empty.

It feels complete.

I sip what's left of my now cold tea—as if trying to
get every last drop out of the night.
The warmth is faint now, but it lingers.
Like a memory I'll carry in my chest,
long after the words are gone.

Ram Dass sits quietly, palms resting open.
Adler's gaze drifts to the window, where the first
gold begins to thread the horizon.

Outside, the night is giving way.

Not with a crash.

With a bow.

Like it knows it's done its part. And what a part
it was.

The fire has faded to embers,
but its heat still pulses in the center of the room.

No more masks.
No more questions.
Just breath.

Just the steady return to life.

And somewhere in the distance,
a bird sings once.

Not a chorus.

Just a single note
that says:

You made it.

The dark did not swallow you.
The silence did not undo you.
The breaking did not end you.

You're still here.
More here than ever.

You've died into yourself.

And now—
it's time to live.

Not with urgency.

With reverence.

With bare feet on the earth.
With open hands.
With a name you no longer need to defend.

Not because you've figured it out.
But because you've remembered:

You belong.

To the light.
To the love.
To the whole aching, holy dance of it all.

The morning waits—
and so does whatever comes next.

But for now…
Just this:
The quiet before the sun.
The breath before the page.

The space
before the rest of your life begins.

# CHAPTER TWELVE
## *The Sun Rises*

It happens quietly.

No announcement.
No applause.
No sudden burst of clarity.

Just a soft shift in the dark.
A thinning of night.
A light that doesn't ask to be noticed—
only received.

The fire is almost out now.
Not because it failed.
But because its work is done.

I sit with a cup in my hands—
empty now.
And I realize…

So am I.

Not empty from loss.
Empty like a field before the bloom.
Like a page before the poem.
Like a heart before the next yes.

Ram Dass hasn't spoken in some time.
Adler either.
But they're still here.
Present.
Whole.
Unhurried.

No more questions.
No more teaching.
Just…being.

I look toward the window.
And I see it—
the first brushstroke of light on the edge of the
horizon.
Not loud.
Not bright.
But true.

And something inside me stands up,
even before my body does.

Not because it's time to leave.
But because it's time to live.

I press my palms to the floor—steady, cool.
My legs unfold slowly, like a fawn remembering they
work.
A soft breath rises as I stand, not fully knowing who
I am now—only that I'm not who I was.

The light through the window has shifted. I feel it on
my skin.

It's quiet, but not still. Something in me has begun to move.

Not as the person I was when I entered this room—
but as the one who is still being revealed.

The one who doesn't need to shine to be seen.
Or speak to be heard.
Or achieve to be worthy.

Just breathe.
Just love.
Just belong.

To this moment.
To this place.
To this life.

The fire didn't give me new answers.
It gave me new eyes.

The world outside hasn't changed.
The ache still exists. The questions remain.
But I am not who I was.

And maybe that's the miracle.
That nothing had to be fixed—
for everything to feel different.

I used to think I needed a bigger life.
More impact. More meaning.
But maybe I just needed a truer one.
Not built from ambition—
but from alignment.

Not about being seen—
but about being here.
And so, I rise.
Not with grandeur.
Not with fanfare.
But with willingness.
To begin again.
To carry this light forward.

To let creation be my prayer.
And my life—my offering.

∞

And for a moment, I don't speak.

I just look around the room—really look.

The fire, low now, but still glowing.
Thank you for your warmth.
For your patience.
For holding our words without judgment.

The breeze slips through the cracked window—cool
and clean.
Thank you for your breath.
For reminding us we are not separate from the
world that moves around us.

The trees outside—tall, still, listening.
Thank you for keeping watch.
For witnessing our becoming.

For holding the silence long enough for truth to speak.

The stars, fading now into the light.
Thank you for staying.
For whispering your quiet wisdom
while we remembered who we are.

I look at Ram Dass.
I look at Adler.

No one needs to say anything more.

And maybe that's the greatest gift of all—
to leave a sacred night not with a conclusion,
but with a blessing.

A soft bow to everything that held us.
Everything that stayed.
Everything that spoke without needing words.

I rise, slowly.

Not to leave.

But to live.

# EPILOGUE
## *The Starry Night Within*

I don't know what brought you to this book.
Maybe heartbreak. Or exhaustion. Or some quiet
ache you've never been able to name.
Maybe it was longing. Or restlessness.
Or a flicker of light you haven't let yourself believe in
for years.

Whatever it was—
I'm glad you came.

I imagine it was something soft and sacred inside
you, asking to be heard again.
Not by me.
Not by the world.
But by you.

This story was never really about the narrator.
Or Ram Dass.
Or Alfred Adler.
Or even the fire.

It was about you.
About all of us.

This book wasn't written to impress.
It was written to remind.
To reflect something you already know.
Something you've maybe always known.

That you are not too much.
That you are not too far.
That you have never needed to become someone else
to be worthy of love.

That being in love isn't about romance.
It's a state of being.
A way of walking.
A willingness to show up soft
when the world tells you to be sharp.

So may you remember your soul.
And return to it often.

May we all have the courage to feel.
The willingness to belong.
And the audacity to believe
that something as simple as a book—or a
conversation, or a moment of truth—

Can change the world.

And maybe, just maybe...
we were never trying to become anything at all.
We were only ever trying to remember.

That we are not separate.
Not small.
Not lost.

We are stars wrapped in skin.